Prodigal Daughter

a memoir

VICKI HARLEY HOLLAND

credo
house publishers

CONTENTS

One Sunday early in the new year of 1934, two daughters were born to women who shared a room in an Allentown, Pennsylvania, hospital. In the corridor outside, the two new fathers were getting acquainted. The one asked the other, "Have you decided on a name for your daughter?"

My father said he had not.

"Well, would you consider the name Vera? I think it's a beautiful name but I don't dare suggest it to my wife. She'd kill me, because it's my secretary's name."

And that's how I became Vera Weiss.

Vera, age 12, 1946

VERA

Mizpah Grove, Allentown

Weiss family, 1939

❧ CHAPTER ONE

I awoke that morning remembering the intense quarrel of the previous night—my mother yelling and driving me mad enough to want to run away. After she left my room, I dragged a small suitcase out of the closet and packed in as many of my favorite items as would fit. I had planned to wake early and quietly creep down to the passageway next to our house and hide the suitcase until it was time to leave for school. I'd leave as any other day, then turn left instead of right, and walk to the train station and head for New York.

But I had the unfortunate characteristic of feeling fresh and forgiving each time I awoke. It was as if all the ugliness of the previous day was washed from my memory—if not from my memory, from my wanting to do something about it, to get even. It no longer mattered. That part of me was irritating, because I could never seem to follow through with my resolve. Nothing ever got dealt with.

So my first thought this morning was *How ridiculous of me to have thought I'd run away* . . . and I turned over and dozed some more. Finally I snapped on my radio and was listening to some pop music when my mother rushed in the door as if she were warning that the house was on fire. She immediately snapped off the dial and glared at me angrily. "You are *not* to turn on that

3

music in the morning until you have read a chapter of the Bible, is that clear?"

Suddenly the tumult of the previous evening overwhelmed me like a flood. The flight was "on" again! However, it was now too late to smuggle my case into the passageway. I'd have to leave without it.

I slipped out the front door carrying only a shoulder bag with a precious few items and twenty-five dollars. I had saved about fifteen dollars and augmented this amount with a ten dollar bill from my father's missionary box stored on a shelf near the kitchen door. I figured this would keep me until I found a job.

I nervously approached the ticket office at the train station, trying hard to look sophisticated and blasé as I said, "One way to New York." I hoped he would not remember me. I hoped I looked older.

"That'll be five dollars and forty-four cents."

As I paid for my ticket, I was saying good-bye to Allentown forever. I was just fourteen years old.

I had lived my own private life for a few years at that point. The family was often a nuisance, an interference. My older sister, Irene, was forever watching me—in church across the auditorium, observing whenever I misbehaved, whispered, drew caricatures and giggled with friends. Then after church she'd zoom across the auditorium, grab my mother's attention, and whisper of all the dreadful things I'd done. I would be in for it that day. Maybe not a physical punishment, but one far worse—my mother's endless tongue-lashing, which was much more painful than a brief slap.

When I was seven years old and taking advanced classes as a

pupil in a nearby "Opportunity School," I rubbed shoulders with boys and girls who lived in a different world than mine. Many were Catholics (a terrible sin) and others Lutheran or Jewish or nothing at all. They had their own cliques and their own parties and exciting lives. None of them were Mennonites. They had no idea what a restricted world I lived in. I so envied them their parties and dances and movies. It was amazing to think of parents who would allow their children to do such things! I felt like I was an outcast and was very lonely.

By the time I was twelve, I decided to mutiny. I chose a Saturday night when my parents were otherwise occupied, and my sister was off at the Mennonite Youth Club or a similar boring event. I walked into town, to the Rialto Theater, and with my heart beating so wildly that I could hardly breathe, I followed the line to the little booth in front and asked for a ticket. I didn't know who Van Johnson or June Allyson was. I had never heard of the film *High Barbaree*. But when I entered that dark theater and saw a new world unfolding on that vast screen, I was hooked. What a glorious sight! I wept as the couple was separated and again when they were reunited. I watched in awe as they kissed—a sight that had me spellbound. To think of such a thing happening to me!

From then on, I always managed to make up some excuse to go "into town," to "visit Mary Jane," or just to "take a walk." I was able to slip out at least once a week, but eventually became so proficient (or brazen) that I would go to the movies as many as three times a week. A favorite practice was to go to Tuesday night prayer meeting, give my requisite testimony early on in the meeting, and then slip out the back door and head for the Gordon Theater, a few blocks away. Sometimes my parents didn't notice and I'd be back mingling with the church members at a quarter after nine when the meeting usually broke up. Other times my mother would say, "Where were you? I saw you leaving!" and I'd casually say I had a tummy upset and went downstairs to the basement ladies' room where I remained until I felt better. It always seemed to suffice.

Of course all this subterfuge took a toll on my relations within the family. It was downright uncomfortable each time I'd hurry home, wondering whether someone had caught me walking into a movie and telephoned my mother to pass on the news. Would she be waiting for me at the door, ready to give me another tongue-lashing? Would she sulk for days as my punishment, refusing to talk to me, or give me that disapproving glare that sent shivers throughout my body? Would Irene come home someday, triumphantly reporting to Mother what dreadful things she heard about me?

But there is no doubt that my private life had irrevocably begun on the night I sneaked out of the house, met a neighbor named Harold Binder on the corner, and stepped into his brand-new 1946 black Chrysler sedan. We had whispered together for a few weeks now. I'd sit on the front porch, waiting for him to pull up, and he'd get out of the car and come up to me, leaning over the porch railing. He was tall and big, with a bouncy, cocky gait. He looked much older than nineteen to my twelve-year-old eyes—so exciting it made my head spin.

He was not only handsome, he showed a great interest in my life. I was able to tell him about the restrictions in my home and in my church. He encouraged me to enjoy myself and go to the movies whenever I wanted. He thought I should learn to dance, but I was too self-conscious for that. He commiserated with me about my strict parents and my narrow life. I was touched by his concern and sympathy, and I was sure I was in love with him.

One day he suggested that we go for a drive that night. I reminded him that my parents would never agree. And then he offered a possibility that terrified me. "When do your parents go to bed? You could wait until they are asleep and then creep out."

I was trembling at the thought. Would it be possible? They were usually in bed by ten, certainly asleep by eleven. And so we agreed to meet just after eleven that night. My heart was in my throat for the rest of the day.

I crept out of bed and dressed quietly, carefully tiptoeing down the stairs. At the front door, I knew there was no turning back. I could see his car parked across the street and the dark shadow of him behind the wheel, a white speck from his cigarette beckoning me. And then he leaned over and opened the door to me.

We drove along Lehigh Parkway in total darkness. I was too excited to speak. Finally he pulled into a spot under some trees and parked the car. His arm slid along the back of my seat. The terror and excitement grew. And then he kissed me! I remembered June Allyson, swept into Van Johnson's arms, but this was *me*! I was loved, appreciated, and admired!

And then his hand slipped up my leg under my skirt and I didn't know what to do. This was something different, and I didn't know what to say. I wanted him to love me, and yet . . .

"You don't understand," he was saying. "You know your parents are wrong to not allow you to go to movies and dances. Well this is just like that . . ."

I know what happened next, and yet I don't remember it. I have tried all these years to remember it, but it is blacked out and I cannot retrieve it. I don't remember him starting up the car and driving me back home. I don't remember a word he said to me then or my reply. I don't remember saying good-bye to him when he dropped me off or quietly opening the front door.

The next thing that I remember is standing in the bathroom, looking in the mirror at my eyes. I looked and looked into them, trying to understand what had happened. Why did it go wrong?

After that, my life became even more of a secret. I dared not tell my parents; it was unthinkable. I could not tell any of my friends either. It was a shock to my system that has never left me. There was only one person that found out—Ronnie. He was a guy of fourteen, who had a crush on me, and we would talk from time to time. After the Lehigh Parkway night, he told me that Harold was on a street corner with some of his friends, laughing and talking about me, about what he had done.

Ronnie wasn't strong enough to fight Harold, so his only weapon was to report those terrible words to me. That was the second assault. And Harold never spoke to me again.

There was still school, still studies, still good times with girl-friends, and still the movies. Mother wasn't always angry, and Irene wasn't always tattling. My father was a quiet man, loving, never condemning. I existed in this private world of mine, and it wasn't all bad. But the damage Harold did to me grew and grew over those early years and it became like a computer virus, distorting messages and threatening to wipe out valuable memories. Above all, it caused a malfunction in my relationships, in what I considered acceptable or unacceptable. I had lost the ability to discern. I had been programmed that night to behave in such a way and from then on, that seemed to be the only way I knew.

CHAPTER TWO

The snowy streets of New York were crowded with commuters and visitors as on any normal day. To me it seemed like Christmas, all the shops and lights and movie theaters beckoning temptingly. For the first time in my life, I could walk into a movie without fear that my parents or friends from my church might be passing by and would see what I was doing. I was finally free to go or do whatever I wanted! That is, as long as my funds held out.

But first there was the small matter of a job. I went into one small shop after another, asking for work. I was rebuffed in each, but in a confectionery store the woman asked, "Do you have a Social Security card?" I hadn't thought about that. She advised me to go to the Social Security office a few blocks away and apply for one.

I filled out a form with my name, birth date, and address. I had always hated the name Vera. Now I could become someone new, and so my new name, I decided, was Elizabeth Gennis. I can't recall what address I gave. Within an hour, I obtained a card which confirmed that I was sixteen years old and able to work. But after all that job hunting and official business, I decided to reward myself with a double feature movie and think about further options.

It didn't seem likely that I'd find a room that night, and since New York theaters at that time were open for twenty-four hours, I figured I could sleep fairly well in one of the plush seats. I lost myself in the drama of the film, in the sleek elegance of Lizabeth Scott and in the dangerous presence of Burt Lancaster. How I longed to live in such a world! There was an illuminated clock at the exit sign, which I tried not to watch. The day had turned into night, and I still had not eaten more than a few snacks. I did not like the idea of sitting in this seat all night. Perhaps sleeping in the theater wasn't such a good idea. What if someone should come and make me leave?

I began to wish that an older person—man or woman— might take me to their home to stay for a while. If only I knew someone to help me get started! I was aware of the dangers of "white slavery" from the pamphlets I'd read at church and how evil men snatched young girls to work as slaves for them. But the man sitting next to me seemed harmless enough. And when he began to speak to me, I felt some hope. Finally, he said, "Would you like to go to dinner with me after the movie?"

Wasn't this just what I was hoping for? But something caused me to say a firm "no."

He slid closer still and coaxed me. Then he put his hand on my leg.

In a voice I never recognized, I said, "If you don't stop that, I will call the manager."

The clock at the exit sign pointed to nine o'clock.

One hundred miles away, in Allentown, my mother, father, and our pastor, Rev. Musselman, were in our living room, praying on their knees. They were praying for my safety when suddenly

Rev. Musselman got up from his knees. "She's all right now."
It was exactly nine o'clock.

The man slunk away up the aisle, turning back to look at me just once. Suddenly the horror of what I'd just escaped dawned on me. I waited for some minutes and then I too left my seat and walked to the back of the theater. In the last row, I spied a middle-aged woman, sitting alone. I said, "May I ask you a question?"

I gave her an abridged version of my grief at home and also modified it somewhat by saying that I was sixteen and my parents knew I was leaving. I can recall all these years later that she said "even a strict home is better than no home at all." Perhaps I was beginning to accept the wisdom of those words. But still I hoped that she would invite me back to her home, whatever it was.

Instead she began to tell me how desperately worried my parents would be by now. And she suggested going with me to the policeman on the corner. I saw there was no other option, and we got up and left the theater.

The big Irish cop leaned down to talk to me amidst all the clamor and crowding on Forty-Second and Broadway. He listened as my new friend suggested that I'd "sort of run away."

"And how old are you?" he asked, hunched over with his big hands on his knees.

"Sixteen."

He put his face nearer to mine. "How old?" he asked again.

"Fourteen."

"Tha-at's better." We thanked the lady who then disappeared out of my life, having been in those few moments God's messenger and deliverer.

The cop and I rode the bus to a juvenile shelter some blocks away, and he put me into the care of staff there who showed me to a bed in an empty ward. One of them phoned my parents to tell them where I was, and our neighbor Mr. Suter agreed to drive up to collect me the following day. My father did not yet own an automobile.

CHAPTER THREE

"Now may I go to movies?" I asked my mother soon after my return. I was determined to get into a good bargaining position. They were doing their best trying to accommodate me, but this was too much.

"I'd rather see you dead than go to the movies."

It was a comment I was able to use to advantage with friends who were not of my church background. People were aghast that I was so ill-treated. In truth, I was loved, but my parents simply did not know how to deal with such a difficult daughter. My older sister, Irene, was day to my night. She had always been submissive, obedient, dutiful to both parents and church. She worked hard at school and her free time was spent with her Mennonite friends. She hadn't given the family a moment's worry. Why then, they must have wondered, was I such a rebel?

I gingerly returned to my obsession with the movies. I bought movie magazines and learned all about the stars. I became emboldened to use every opportunity to see as many films as possible. By the late 1940s, more and more movies were in Technicolor. Many a winter afternoon I would leave the theater and the dazzling colorful scenes therein to walk home along cold gray streets, through rain or slush or snow—a gray world that I had grown to hate—longing instead to climb into the cinema screens and be a part of those glorious Technicolor stories. I recall watching a film in color called *Good News*, a collegiate story starring Peter Lawford and June Allyson. How I craved to be part of that dazzling world, instead of my miserable life!

I remember a happy early childhood. I still have a photo of myself, a laughing three-year-old, sitting astride a pony at the corner of Eighth and Washington Streets in Allentown. I recall that day: I had a bruise on my knee from a recent fall, and I so hoped that my bruise, my badge of honor, would show on the photo. And it did!

I felt I was a privileged child for many years. My father, a keen musician, sensed my own musical talent at an early age. I sang a solo at our church camp meeting when only four years old. The next year my father taught Irene and me to sing in harmony. I sang alto to Irene's soprano, and the harmony came easily to me. He then taught us to memorize hymns, three verses and chorus of each. I was quick to memorize and often learned the songs before nine-year-old Irene did. That would annoy her.

Before long we were not only singing regularly as the Weiss Sisters in our own Bethel Mennonite Church, but we began to receive invitations to sing in other churches in the area and finally further afield in Pennsylvania and New Jersey. We often sang on the Bethel Church radio programs on Allentown's WSAN Sunday nights. We sang at conferences and special rallies. I was still a tiny child with Shirley Temple curls, while my sister was by now a plump ten-year-old, with a straight bobbed hairdo. My mother dressed us in identical dresses often with little velvet sashes and ribbon bows in our hair. People murmured their pleasure after a song and often made a particular fuss of me, the little one. I enjoyed that, and I enjoyed singing to appreciative audiences.

My mother kept a tight rein on us even as we sang. She would sit in a pew visible to us, and her body language told us how well we were doing. If she rubbed her left ear as we sang, the child standing on the left wasn't singing loudly enough. If she rubbed the right side of her mouth, the child on the right had better turn down the volume. Her severe face and movements controlled us as effectively as any conductor could do.

In time we learned several hundred hymns; many of these I have remembered all my life. Those early years gave us many opportunities to visit other homes and other churches. One day we sang at a nearby Nazarene church. That is how I learned finally that Mennonites were not the only Christians. It broadened my outlook somewhat.

Soon afterward, I asked my mother, "How can you tell whether a church is Christian or not?"

She said, "Well, if they say the Lord's Prayer, they're not Christian."

Among my happy childhood memories were those of Daily Vacation Bible School (DVBS), sometimes held at our church, sometimes in other Allentown churches. I loved the memorizing of Bible verses, psalms, and chapters. I loved the sword drills, finding the Bible passages first and winning prizes. When I was eleven, the DVBS in a nearby church offered a special prize for the student gaining the highest amount of points—ten days at Camp Sunshine in Waldheim Park. The night my name was called was one of the happiest of my childhood. And the camp experience was a wonderful one.

But most of all, memories of childhood are focused on Mizpah Grove, the wooded hilly area east of Allentown where all the Mennonite families in our conference came each summer, to set up camp and spend up to six weeks together. Five hundred canvas tents were erected in rows around a large open-sided pavilion. There was a large prayer tent in which the seats were bales of hay. There was a dining hall across the path, an ice cream stand, a book store and several cement structures higher up the hill for showers and toilets.

Families brought camp cots for sleeping or used wooden pens filled with straw for more rustic beds. Camp chairs and folding tables were adequate for meals taken either inside the tents or outside. Every tent had a small kerosene stove on a little platform just outside. I can still smell the kerosene stoves, the wonderful aroma of a variety of foods cooking all along the paths; and I can hear the rain as it pelted against the canvas of our tents late into the night or cascaded down the sides of the open pavilion as we sang even louder to drown it out. "Showers of blessing" was always a favorite hymn sung heartily when the rains came. I can still see the choir filing in on the platform—grown-up men and women to my young eyes—and hear the pianists pounding those keys as the service commenced.

The heavy schedule of daily services at Mizpah Grove might shock today's churchgoers. There were up to seven services listed every day in the week. I was obliged to attend at least two of these. But services sometimes went on far too long for my young attention span, and I shifted restlessly in my seat, sometimes whispering loudly to my companions sitting with me, sometimes drawing caricatures of the men and women within my sight, causing ripples of laughter or snickers from my friends. But when Irene was able to observe my transgressions, there was a debt to pay. I knew she would dart over to Mother immediately after the final "Amen." By nine o'clock at night I was eager for the last hymn and prayer and already looking longingly at the ice cream stand, waiting for the moment when the serving hatch would be opened and we could rush over for an ice cream.

Today in my library in England, over the bookshelves, hangs an old sepia photograph of Mizpah Grove as it appeared in 1926, with rows of families clustered in front of tents, the scene unchanged for decades. I wasn't born in 1926, but many of the faces remain familiar to me, as younger faces hardly changed in the years to come. I recognize many families, including my own, in that wonderful slice of blissful memory. I wish I could go back to Mizpah Grove, even for an hour. But it's no longer there.

CHAPTER FOUR

My life improved somewhat after my return from New York. It was the year that Irene finished high school and traveled to California to attend Westmont College, where our uncle was a professor of psychology. It took the heat off me, and also I gained the larger bedroom in her absence. Furthermore I enjoyed a new relationship with my cousin Mimi in Philadelphia, whose social life proved more liberal than my own. She and I sometimes visited friends in West Philly whose house was often overrun with young men in their twenties and who apparently existed with no restrictions at all. I marveled at such freedom and couldn't wait for my next visit to Mimi and my next visit to these young people who seemed to live in a state of perpetual partying.

Toward the end of that school year, I learned that my high school basketball team was playing a West Philly team, and a bus would take any students who wanted to travel to Philly for the game. It was a golden opportunity for me to spend a few hours in that house with the gang I so admired. I couldn't have cared less about basketball. I'd simply slip away from the school group and take the elevated train across the city to visit my new friends.

It was always an open house there, and no one raised an eyebrow when I walked through the door and sat down. There was pop music on the radio and a cloud of cigarette smoke hanging low in the room. Bliss! The hours passed far too quickly and soon I knew I'd have to return to the stadium in a hurry to catch the bus back to Allentown.

When I arrived at the designated spot, however, there was no bus anywhere. And no students! In fact the premises were in darkness, and with dread I realized that I had been too late for the bus back to Allentown. What could I do? I had no money, having spent my last coins on the transport to West Philly. I didn't even have enough to make a phone call! I stood outside a gas station, frantic with worry, wondering how I could get home.

After a few moments, two truck drivers came up to me, asking if they could help. I explained my dilemma and they offered me a way out. They were going to Allentown that night and would give me a lift! I could not thank them enough. We piled into their cab, with me in the middle, and were away. They asked my name and I asked theirs. I was surprised that they said they were both called "Ike."

As we approached Allentown, the elder pulled the lorry over to the side and said something about having to get out. It was the cue for the younger "Ike" to slip his arm around the back of the seat and try to lower me to the seat. Suddenly I thought of Harold Binder and I straightened up. "No, you don't!" I said firmly. At that moment I looked up and saw the driver peering through the window. "You can come in now," I called to him, "because nothing is going to happen!"

I had no idea what a dangerous game this might have been. I did not realize that I might have been just another statistic, a body found the following morning, and the truckers long gone into another state. I was just thankful when they drove me home and actually dropped me at my door.

But a day later my mother was told by another parent that

I was missing from the bus on the return home. She immediately called our new pastor, Rev. Miller, who came to the house to question me about it. Neither my mother nor my pastor believed me when I explained that I'd missed the bus and accepted an innocent ride with two truckers. I finally admitted that the one had tried to force himself on me, but that I resisted him. They didn't believe this either.

Rev. Miller decided that I needed to publicly confess in church the following Sunday evening. I was to walk up to the altar at the end of the service when an invitation was given. Refusing wasn't an option. And so that next Sunday night, Easter Sunday, I walked to the front, knelt down, and looked as contrite as possible.

I'd had a lucky escape, but a foolish young girl doesn't always learn from her deceptions. There were times in the coming years that I didn't escape the consequences of my folly. Often I described that incident as a gross injustice of having to "confess" to something I didn't do. But there were plenty of times that I lied and cheated and yet didn't get discovered. I never considered the injustice of *that*.

CHAPTER FIVE

In my senior year of high school, I applied for a job at Sears Roebuck nearby. My sister had previously worked part-time at Sears during her senior year and summers to finance her time at college. For the princely sum of sixty-five cents an hour, I was able to take her place in the credit department, working weekends during my final year of high school, holidays, and summers, saving enough for a sizable deposit on my bill for the first year at college. I enjoyed the work, interviewing people for credit accounts, and I enjoyed mingling with young men and women in a business setting. There were also numerous opportunities to join them at local bars and working men's clubs, where I learned how to consume as much alcohol as the next person, despite being only sixteen.

The greatest cause for celebration was the fact that I'd be leaving for California a few months after graduation. I could hardly contain my joy. Of course I was enrolling in a Christian college, with all the rules and regulations of such a place, but photos of the young people attending Westmont convinced me that they were very much more up-to-date than my Mennonite acquaintances. And pictures of the beautiful California coastline, Santa Barbara in particular, made me fall in love with the area.

In September of that year, I said good-bye to the family and boarded a Greyhound bus for the three-and-a-half-day ride across country, with changes of bus in Pittsburgh, St. Louis, Omaha, Denver, and Phoenix. My final transfer was in Los Angeles, where I boarded the last bus to Santa Barbara.

I had decided during the long coach trip that since this was going to be a new life for me, I ought to start off with a new name. I decided that instead of my birth name Vera, Vicki was far more suitable for the person I hoped to become. Although all official papers retained my original name, students and friends accepted my nickname without question. That name swept aside all the miserable associations with the name Vera. In recent years I had come to hate hearing my mother yelling it angrily. In school, some of the Pennsylvania Dutch teachers called me "Wera Veiss," to the amusement and snickers of my fellow classmates. And thanks to a giddy comedienne on the Bob Hope show I was often teasingly called Vera Vague. I wanted to bury that name forever. I couldn't get rid of it fast enough! So in Santa Barbara, at age seventeen, I became Vicki Weiss.

Santa Barbara was a Spanish-style paradise; and the campus, nestled on the exquisite Montecito hillside overlooking the Pacific, was more beautiful than anything I'd ever seen. Better still, within days a handful of rebels in that small community of three hundred students singled out those who were of like minds. It didn't take me long to find other mischievous gals who were determined to break as many rules as possible, who had also come from strict Christian homes and were longing to become independent from them. Together we enjoyed mocking the puritanical types who fell in line with whatever regulations were thrown at them. We soon found the local venues where we could smoke and drink and manage to keep one step ahead of the college authorities. I even managed to meet some local musicians who asked me to solo with them at venues around Santa Barbara, including a cocktail lounge and later a military ball in San Luis Obispo.

But eventually even beautiful Santa Barbara wasn't enough to satisfy me as I longed for that freedom that still eluded me. Friends drove me one hundred miles south to Los Angeles and I soon decided that this was what I was searching for. My heart wasn't really in my studies; I wanted to get a job and earn money, buy a car, have an apartment. Maybe even pursue a musical career. Surely that's where true happiness lay! And with some clever maneuvering, I slipped free of college restraints and planned to move to LA that following autumn.

First I was obliged to return to Pennsylvania for the summer, to work at Sears again to replenish my funds for the coming year. Also to be the maid of honor at my sister's wedding that August. She had transferred to an eastern college for her final two years, and there she met a theology major, Don, studying to be a pastor. It was just what Irene had wanted all her life. I was too self-occupied at the time to give her much thought, but I agreed to be her maid of honor. My thoughts were three thousand miles away, in Los Angeles, with Johnie, a sandy-haired weight lifter who had won my heart. It was my first love, and I could think of nothing else that summer. I loved him so much I was in equal measures deliriously happy and sick with worry and fear.

After three long months away from him, my greatest joy was to step off the Greyhound in LA into his arms. He took me back to his parents' house and I stayed there until we found a small apartment for me, not so far away. I quickly found an office job and those first two months were indescribably happy.

I wasn't even worried when I suspected I was pregnant. It would simply speed up the wedding plans, I thought. But Johnie had other ideas, and I realized with dread that his ardor had quickly cooled. He first insisted on homemade abortion remedies, forcing me to drink large glasses of neat gin and to sit in a near boiling tub of water. It only succeeded in making me terribly ill. Finally he found an abortionist, Dr. Harry of 749 Norton Avenue, a creepy old man who abused me even as he used some electrical equipment to abort the baby. During that whole painful period I learned that Johnie had found another girlfriend and was planning to marry her. Before the abortion and after it, I felt nothing but despair.

Gradually I began partying again—noisy nightclubs were the easiest way of drowning my grief. I drank more and ate less. One day I suffered such violent headaches that I wound up in LA General Hospital. At first diagnosed with meningitis, I was finally found to have contracted polio, during the last epidemic of that dread disease that spread across the country in 1952. I was hospitalized for a week, fortunately only temporarily paralyzed. Two other young women in my room were not so lucky. I returned to my apartment, grateful for that escape, ready to return to work and play as soon as possible.

But a knock on my door changed all that. I opened the door on an old, gray-haired woman and moments later realized it was my mother! She had flown in a plane for the first time in her life and was coming to take me home. She had consulted with the local police department which confirmed that at age eighteen, I must obey her and return home for the next three years or they could take me to juvenile court. The flight back to Allentown was my first trip in an airplane, but it was one of the lowest points in my young life.

CHAPTER SIX

Wat a bitter experience to be returned to the family home in shame! It was as if I had been free on parole, but that one violation put me back in prison again. Of course there were many violations, many bad companions and foolish moves. My parents learned of only some of them. Irene, now a married woman working to put Don through seminary, was furious with me for bringing disgrace on the family. She and Don were a formidable team to stand with my parents in condemning my behavior.

But if I was returned to prison, at least I was permitted daily work release. And where else could I find a suitable environment for my talents than in an all-male college nearby? Muhlenberg College was founded by Lutherans, but was now more of a secular institution than a religious one. Fraternity houses enjoyed plenty of drinking parties and other celebrations. Although I was appointed secretary in the public relations department, I soon got involved with the social side after hours and found myself a boyfriend in the ATO fraternity. So, I decided, there was life after California after all! I had a three-year plan that would take me up to my twenty-first birthday, after which I would be free to go wherever I chose. Although I had found the Mennonite atmosphere suffocating, I now saw there was more to Allentown than that. I could survive at home!

My new boyfriend, Don, was a handsome, dark-haired guy who drove an old 1948 royal-blue Buick convertible. We soon hung out at his favorite bar virtually every night. He and I suited each other: I had my three-year plan and he was not interested in settling down. We each took what we wanted from the relationship and thought it was an ideal arrangement.

We fell into this routine for almost a year but somewhere along the line I was getting fed up. Don loved to shoot darts in a nearby bar and so would pick me up at my house most evenings and take me to Vinnie's Bar on Tilghman Street. There he'd order me a whiskey sour, sit me on a barstool and then disappear to the other end of the room, playing darts with the boys. Occasionally I grumbled, but we usually wound up doing what Don wanted.

One night after a typical evening at Vinnie's, he dropped me at the curb and drove off. I stood in the little patch of lawn in front of our porch and looked up at the stars. I found myself yearning to be free! There was something in my chest that seemed to be reaching to the sky, longing to be clean again, yearning to start over! It surprised me that I should be thinking this way. Wasn't I already free? I stood there for some moments, just looking heavenward.

I didn't identify it at that moment as a prayer, but in the weeks and months to come I realized that it was the first reaching out to God that I had experienced in many a year. The freedom which I had arranged for myself had not been satisfactory. I was providing pleasure for Don, but what was I getting out of life? I worked, came home, lived a fairly peaceable life with my parents, and tried to avoid conflict as much as possible. But now that didn't seem enough.

Several weeks later, I received an answer to that "prayer" that was the last thing in the world I would wish for. I was pregnant.

I knew marriage to Don wasn't the answer. I simply didn't love him, and he didn't love me. In the 1950s we rarely heard of abortions, and abortionists, although one doctor in New York had recently been exposed and sent to prison for the death of a young girl when the operation went wrong. But ordinary young people like Don and me had no means of knowing where to go. He promised to check with his college friends and other contacts for a suitable name and address.

That was in October 1954. I spent the next few months anxiously awaiting word about to what to do. To give birth at this stage of my life was unthinkable. My parents would be devastated. My mother would be furious; my father would be heartbroken. I was beginning to look at myself, the past few years, and my choices, with a new eye. I did not want to hurt them! I did not want this to happen to them!

Finally late in December, Don learned of a doctor in New York who would be willing to perform the abortion. The first week in January we traveled to New York and met up with this unnamed doctor at the Hampshire House Hotel. He examined me and then looked at me in horror. "I can't touch you! You're four months pregnant!"

Although decades later "late-term abortions" were declared legal, in 1955 no sensible doctor would attempt to carry out such a procedure. And that night I realized that I would have to go through with the pregnancy after all. I would have to give birth to this baby.

I was stunned. I could hardly think for days. I could tell no one and somehow even Don and I did not discuss it. The saving grace was that I was approaching my twenty-first birthday, and my mother and father always knew I wanted to return to California when I was twenty-one. Gradually I came to see that I could leave the family home, ostensibly leave Allentown, and go somewhere to have the baby, give it up for adoption, and then perhaps return home afterward. What irony, that I had counted the months and years until I could leave home, and now I was considering returning right after the birth!

That month I began to think of the Salvation Army that had a Corps in Allentown and an adjoining shelter. Might it be possible that they would be willing to take me in? And so one day I took the bus across town, knocked at their door at Eighth and Turner, and was introduced to the Major's wife.

Mrs. Hood was a no-nonsense woman who was used to getting things done without emotion or sentimentality. She listened to my story and then mentioned a couple in the area who were childless and who were hoping to adopt. The wife, she said, was a redheaded nurse, and the couple attended the Lutheran Church. I was fortunate to have even those few details; in those days no information was permitted to the birth mother. I was told a room would be provided for me in the shelter, and I could come whenever I was ready.

I left the Salvation Army that day relieved and grateful, and could now plan for the months ahead. I informed my parents that I'd be returning to California the following week. Instead of a twenty-first birthday celebration, I was driven by Don from my home in West Allentown along Turner Street to the Army building. Only later did I recall a prophetic picture of that journey. When I was fourteen years old, our art class windows looked out onto Turner Street, between Eighth and Ninth Street. Our teacher told us to paint whatever we saw out of those windows. I sketched and then painted the row of houses along Turner Street, bisected by Lumber Street with its tiny row houses stretching to Hamilton. I painted the corner shop with the Freeman's Milk sign on the wall and the chimneys along the rooftops. There was a large single house on the left of my painting, with a brick wall. And then I watched as a 1948 royal-blue Buick convertible went slowly past Lumber Street, and I painted it driving along in the direction of the large, brick building. Seven years later, that picture came to life as Don's 1948 blue Buick convertible drove me to that same building in which my life would change forever.

✦ CHAPTER SEVEN

Once again I was standing in a building on Turner Street, looking out of a window at the life in the street below. This time I was on the opposite side of the one I drew. I watched as children hurried to school each morning or yelped and played during recesses. I watched a young woman wheeling a baby carriage, and it reassured me to think that she survived the ordeal that lay ahead of me. I stood in that attic window and watched for hours, wishing I might warn the carefree teenage girls about choices and dreams.

My attic room was simply furnished with a single bed and dresser on a linoleum covered floor. The room was for sleeping only, even though sleep did not come easily now. During the day I sat in an upstairs sun-room with a pile of old magazines to read. Downstairs, on the ground floor, there was a parlor furnished only with a small black-and-white television set and two wooden dining chairs on a bare floor. The dining room was empty except for four more dining chairs. In the kitchen an old slate sink and stove took up much of the space, and a wooden table with two more chairs sat by the back door. I tried to spend as little time in the kitchen as possible, because when the light was turned on, all the cockroaches rushed as one to the sink and disappeared down the drain. I was terrified of roaches and felt a panic that they might be found on my food.

The anonymous couple that would be adopting my baby supplied me with tins of food once a week in a large paper bag that appeared on the kitchen table. The tins were largely of fruit or vegetables; I don't recall having any fresh meat or fish. But I had sufficient food and was never hungry.

The highlight of each day was when Jane, the young Army lieutenant, arrived back from her chores at the church or within the community. She was only a few years older than I, and her boyfriend Bob was also a lieutenant in the Army. Unlike me, Jane had made wise choices and had nothing to fear. She and Bob planned to marry in due course, but meanwhile, they lived chaste lives.

She kept her distance at first, unsure of what sort of a person I was. Eventually she warmed to me and listened to my story. She wasn't quick to give advice but was helpful if asked. A few weeks after my arrival she offered me some books to read and showed me an old bookcase in the hall that contained other books and Bibles that I might find useful. One caught my eye: Norman Vincent Peale's *The Power of Positive Thinking*. My evangelical background taught me to be suspicious of this "liberal" pastor; but it seemed the most interesting of the other books, so I picked it up.

I sat in the sun-room at the back of the house, enjoying the early spring sun's rays, and began to read. There were inspiring examples of people who suffered misfortunes or who (like me) had "done those things which we ought not to have done." Rev. Peale's advice was simple, and sometimes it seemed shallow. But then he mentioned one who had trouble sleeping and suggested that those with similar problems read the Twenty-third Psalm and say the Lord's Prayer at bedtime. My overactive mind and worries about the future were preventing me from sleeping well, and I took his advice. But then I found myself praying, really praying, for the first time in many years, *O God! If You're there and can hear me at all, give me sleep!*

The following morning, March 15, 1955, I awoke to a strange sensation. It was a feeling of optimism, of hope, that was at great odds with my situation. "Everything's going to be all right!" I wanted to cry out. I waited impatiently all day for Jane to return from her chores, so that I could share this with her. When I told her, she just looked at me and laughed, unable to fathom my words. When Don arrived for his weekly visit a few nights later, I told him, "Everything's going to be all right!" He looked relieved. "What did I tell you, baby? Of course everything's going to be all right!" But he didn't understand at all.

I finished the Peale book and read one or two others. But then I picked up an old Bible and began to read. I read the Psalms, the Gospels, the Epistles. This was familiar territory; from a child I was taught to memorize Scripture. Now, remarkably, so many of those verses and psalms came to mind as I read them. What's more, the meanings were so sharply focused, and touched my heart so profoundly, that I could not explain it. My eyes fell on a verse at the end of Psalm 16: "You will show me the path of life; in Your presence is fullness of joy; at Your right hand are pleasures forevermore" (v. 11).

How wonderful! I wanted to cry for the beauty and reality of the verse! I had memorized that verse almost fifteen years earlier and had not given it another thought until that spring day. Now it was so precious I could only marvel. All those years I was given the impression that living a life for God meant following rules and regulations, and above all, taking care to *not* do a host of pleasurable things! Now I was seeing another possibility— that living in God's presence could be the highest form of joy! Could this really be true?

The following day I read Psalm 121 and remembered every

word: "I will lift up my eyes to the hills—from whence comes my help? My help comes from the Lord, Who made heaven and earth" (vv.1–2). Oh what a glorious comfort those words were to my soul! To think of that and other Scriptures tucked away in my memory bank all those years, unused, unappreciated, when they could have been a "lamp to my feet and a light to my path" (Ps. 119:105)! I wept over that and other Scriptures, even as I recalled my mother insisting that I read a chapter of the Bible before turning on my radio every morning. How I hated her and her threats at the time! But why had she not shown me the side of "joy" to her faith, rather than the dogmas and condemnation? I was puzzled about that.

And still I didn't know what had happened to me. One thing I knew: it was no longer a pleasure to have Don visit me each Wednesday evening and take me to the drive-in theater. Even though it was the only time in the week that I dared leave the shelter, for fear someone might see me, I no longer saw any value in that weekly "date" with him. After all, Don was history. I knew that even more now.

The following Wednesday I was tempted to suggest that he not come anymore, but then I thought perhaps we could spend one final night at the drive-in movie. At one point he left the car to get some sodas. I needed a paper hankie and looked in his glove compartment to see if I could find one. To my disgust I saw a pack of condoms there! I was furious. How dare that swine do such things when I was in this condition? I fumed for a few minutes, but when he returned, I didn't feel it was worth mentioning. After all, it was over. Perhaps that discovery made it even easier to sever the ties.

Those days I thought a great deal about my parents, and it was becoming clear just how dreadfully I had behaved all those years. What a trial I must have been! Yes, my mother often got angry. She threatened and sulked for days. But my father always looked at me so lovingly, if sadly. It was his face that was ever before me now. How bitterly I regretted my years of folly!

I had been carrying on a sham correspondence with them since leaving their home. I was in touch with Beverly, my old roommate from Los Angeles, and had asked a favor of her. I sent her letters in double envelopes, written to my parents, in need of a California postmark. I didn't give her details but said I wanted to be on my own for a few months, and I didn't want them to know where I was. She obliged me and sent them on their round trip to my home, just a few streets away. They in turn sent replies to her address which she forwarded back to me. All of this subterfuge seemed innocent enough at the start of my confinement, but now a twinge of guilt made me uneasy. Deceit upon deceit, I thought. I was now eager to tell my parents that something good had happened to me and that I was reading the Bible and praying for the first time in years. *Would they believe me?* I wondered.

I wanted very much to stop all the dishonesty that had been a cornerstone of my life for so many years. But I could not believe that it would be helpful to drag my heartbroken parents through this latest trial. I was willing to deal with it on my own and just give them the minimum of details. When I returned home—afterward—they would see I was genuinely determined to change my life for good.

After much thought, I wrote them a brief letter, saying that I had reached a crisis in my life, and I was now reading the Bible and I wanted to make them proud of me again. I added that I planned to return home in the summer. I hoped that would suffice, and I also hoped that on my return I would not have to lie about what had transpired in the months I'd been away.

It was shortly after sending this "round trip" letter that I came upon a revelation. As I slowly read through Paul's letter to the Corinthians, I suddenly came upon the answer to what had happened to me: "Therefore, if anyone is in Christ, he is a new creation; old things have passed away; behold, all things have become new."

That's it, I cried. I have become a new creature in Christ! The discovery was like a thunderbolt to my heart. I recalled the words of Jesus about being "born again" and it all made sense now. It was true that the old had passed away, and I was finding so much that was new and wonderful.

But then a new puzzle surfaced. What about the time I went down to the altar at the Mennonite church when I was five? I had said I wanted to give my heart to Jesus then. Wasn't that the time I was "born again"? All those years that I memorized Scriptures and got awards for it, won every sword drill for finding the verses quickly, and sang hundreds of hymns with Irene? What did that mean? Wasn't I saved then? I even asked to be baptized at the age of seven and had a photo of me coming out of the Jordan River in Allentown. How could I not have been saved at that time?

There weren't too many people I could talk to about this. I could only go back to what Jesus said in the Gospels and try to find my answers there. I saw something in the parable of the sower that made me feel that some make a commitment at one time, but the roots don't go deep enough, and they don't keep their promise to God. Certainly, thinking of all the times I'd gravitated to the very worst sort of person and been drawn to the most unsavory situations, I did not have my roots in God. I deceived parents, family, teachers, pastors. I pretended even as a child to be a little angel when I was far from that. I was ashamed of my parents' faith and my birthright. As a child of eight or nine, I mocked my church to the little Catholic and Jewish classmates who called me a "holy roller." I didn't want to be associated with Mennonite fanatics. I preferred siding with those who mocked me, my parents, and my Lord.

It was good for me to turn over such questions in my mind. It made me return to the Bible for the answers and not seek the help or opinions of others.

In the Psalms I found an abundance of verses that might have been describing my predicament. Psalm 119 was a cry to God from King David, who lamented his sins and failures, but then he looked heavenward and realized that his merciful Lord would use every situation to set him on the right path. "Before I was afflicted I went astray," David wrote, "but now I keep Your Word . . . It is good for me that I have been afflicted, that I may learn Your statutes . . . How sweet are Your words to my taste, sweeter than honey to my mouth! . . . Your word is a lamp to my feet and a light to my path" (Ps. 119:67, 71, 103, 105).

In an old well-worn hymnbook in the hall bookcase, I found a hymn by Charles Wesley that contained a perfect description of what had happened to me that day in March 1955.

Long my imprisoned spirit lay,
Fast bound in sin and nature's night;
Thine eye diffused a quickening ray—
I woke, the dungeon flamed with light;
My chains fell off, my heart was free,
I rose, went forth, and followed Thee!

from "And Can It Be That I should gain?" (1738)

And it seemed that in the following month I was given a crash course of Bible study by the Holy Spirit which prepared me for the rest of my life.

CHAPTER EIGHT

O ne morning toward the end of April I was in my usual place in the upstairs sun-room, reading the Bible. I heard a commotion in the hallway at the foot of the stairs, with Mrs. Hood protesting loudly, and another voice saying, "I know she's here!" To my horror I realized it was my mother's voice! My heart thumped wildly as I heard footsteps ascending to the sun-room. Mrs. Hood stood in the doorway. "I'm sorry, Vicki, but your parents are here. They found out where you were staying. You'll have to go down and talk to them." My dreams of keeping all this mess from them were shattered in that moment. I could not understand why this had to happen, but I knew I had to face the music.

As I walked down the steps, I saw my tearful parents at the bottom—with their arms outstretched! I fell into them, and with our arms round each other, we wept, with that little unplanned life suspended within the circle. All I could say was, "I'm so sorry . . . I'm so sorry!"

And then Daddy said to me, "We'd like you to come home." It made me weep even more. To think of such love and forgiveness when I had made their life a misery for all those years!

After we were all cried out, we sat together and began to talk. I told them I felt I ought to remain in the shelter rather

than expose them—and myself—to any talk in the neighborhood, if someone should see me. I told them I had adjusted to
my quiet life there, and that it was good for me. I was reading
the Bible constantly and learning so much that I had not seen
and understood before. I sensed at once that they accepted what
I said as the truth. I said I would be glad to come home quietly
each weekend, on a Friday night after dark, and return to the
shelter on a Sunday night. This was agreed.

The house that formerly had been a joyless convenience for
me now became a loving refuge. My mother made all my favorite foods and treated me with more tenderness than ever before.
My father's quiet, gentle faith was like the breath of God to me.
Those few days at the end of the week were a treasure I would
never forget.

I gathered from my mother that Irene and Don had been
told, but they did not want to see me until it was "all over."
Mother mentioned to Irene that I had made a new commitment
to the Lord, but she implied that Irene made no comment about
that. I guess my sister was taking a "wait and see" approach.

The final week or two I decided to remain at the shelter, and
one Sunday afternoon my father came to visit me for a few hours.
We sat in the near-empty dining room, on two wooden dining
chairs, holding hands and whispering together. Suddenly a pain
ripped through me, and I sensed that my time had come. My
dearest Daddy put his arm around me and prayed a beautiful
prayer for God to bless and protect me and strengthen me for the
time ahead. He committed me to the One who nurtures the fa-
therless and never leaves nor forsakes those who call upon Him.

A little girl I named Donna Lynn Roberts was born later
that day in a hospital in the next town. I had been told the baby
would be removed immediately so that I wouldn't see it. But a
short time after the birth I was shocked when a nurse brought a

little bundle to my bedside for me to bottle-feed! I looked down into that bundle with awe at the most exquisite little face I'd ever seen. Many newborns are hardly a thing of beauty, with red scrunched up faces. But this one was perfectly formed, with lovely ivory skin and a gorgeous rosebud mouth. She didn't cry once during the five days I remained in the hospital and fed her every day. I often kept her for precious moments after the feeding and sat by the window with her in my arms, praying God's blessing and protection upon her, as my father did for me before her birth. I often held her, remembering the many Scripture passages that now filled my mind and heart . . .

I will lift up my eyes to the hills—
From whence comes my help?
My help comes from the LORD,
Who made heaven and earth.
He will not allow your foot to be moved;
He who keeps you will not slumber.
Behold He who keeps Israel
Shall neither slumber nor sleep. (Ps. 121:1–4)

Such glorious promises that flooded my soul I prayed would enter my daughter's heart and life in future years. I was committing her to another set of parents, yes, but more than that, I was committing her to my Lord. I could not doubt that He had been with me in all of my rebellion. "I will never leave you nor forsake you" (Heb. 13:5) was a promise in my thoughts constantly.

On the fifth day, I packed up my things and prepared to return *home*. It would be a totally new chapter in my life. I could not have imagined, that cold January day when I left the house on Tilghman Street, that I would return less than six months later with such a burden lifted! A miracle had taken place—I had reached out and touched the Lord, and in so doing, He had healed me!

But first I was told we had to make a detour to a lawyer's office. I was accompanied by a nurse who held my daughter as we sat in the back of the car. I can only describe my state at the time as feeling positively lifted up by the Lord, convinced that this was the path I was to take, and that He was leading me. I looked down at that precious bundle next to me and loved her, but I did not grieve.

We sat in the small office, with Attorney Joseph behind his desk, Mrs. Hood nearby, and the nurse holding my baby standing behind my chair. All went well until quite suddenly someone nodded, and the nurse stooped down and put her into my arms. It was such a shock that the precious bundle felt as heavy as a stone. I sobbed for a moment, and then, confused, I lifted her back into the arms of the nurse. Then the attorney motioned with a pen for me to sign a document. What was that all about? What a tactless, cruel thing to do to me!

I understood that I was only signing preliminary papers but that the final document would be signed eight months later. With that, we left the office for the drive back to the shelter where my father picked me up.

CHAPTER NINE

My parents and I agreed that if at all possible we would not have to say anything untruthful about my time away from home. As it turned out, many people from the church and other friends and neighbors only wanted to know "Are you glad to be home?" and not "What were you doing out there?" Not a single person referred to the months I had been in hiding nor questioned me about them. My parents and I were convinced that the Lord was helping me to speak only of the positive side of my absence. We felt that was the grace of God at work once again.

Our pastor came to visit and although I did not feel the need to tell him the details of my months away, I was able to speak in detail of the wonderful change in my heart and life as I knew without a shadow of doubt that I was a "new creature in Christ." He asked me to share my testimony with the congregation the following Sunday, and I gladly agreed.

How I hated going to church all those years! I recalled many a New Year's Eve "Watchnight Service" when I was compelled to sit for hours in those dreary services, singing old hymns, hearing prayers and testimonies! Finally at midnight when distant horns were blown and fireworks set off, I was kneeling at an old oak pew, longing to be out there where real life was going on!

I remembered a time sitting with Don in a cocktail lounge

less than a year earlier, when I suddenly said to him, "Sometimes I think I'm going to wind up back in those Tuesday night prayer meetings . . ." And he laughed and said, "Don't worry about that, baby; you're not the type!"

But I *was* "the type!" I was learning that God had His hand on me long before I reached out and asked for His help. He had His hand on me even before I went up to the altar as a child of five. He had His hand on me before my parents went up to the pastor with me in their arms, at my dedication service. Maybe it was irrelevant as to when I became that new creature in Christ. Recently I had looked at a Scripture that referred to the mystery of those who are in the kingdom and have had their names written in the Book of Life *before the worlds were formed.* "I saw you before you were in your mother's womb," God said to King David (Psalm 139:15–16). Jesus left eternity for a brief moment to enter time and Earth for our sakes. And through His death, we have been bought with the precious blood of Christ and have had our names written in His book before time began. Yes, I was indeed "the type!" Not because of my superiority or righteousness—oh far from it!—but because of His mercy and my earnest appeal to Him.

As I climbed up to the platform to stand behind the pulpit and speak to that large congregation the next Sunday morning, all I could see were loving faces lifted up to me. I explained that I had a sudden revelation of God's love and forgiveness that changed my life. I saw people wipe away tears, and others nodded or said "amen" as I spoke. Afterward people came up to me—many I knew, others I did not—and thanked me for what I shared. "I've prayed for you for nine years!" one woman told me tearfully. How could I have despised those dear people all that time?

My sister and Don had come home from Philadelphia that weekend and were silent around the dinner table that afternoon.

I was still greatly moved by the experience and I sensed my parents were too. After the meal, Irene went to my father and complained. "Why is everyone making such a fuss about Vicki after what she has done? Everyone is celebrating her coming back when I've never gone away in the first place. I've not done all the awful things she did, but she's the one that gets all the glory!"

Daddy quietly directed her to read the story of the Prodigal Son once again and reminded her of the other brother who had faithfully remained at home. Yes he had been the "good" son, but he too greatly resented the fact that everyone was celebrating the return of the Prodigal.

> "He answered and said to his father, 'Lo, these many years I have been serving you; I never transgressed your commandment at any time; and yet you never gave me a young goat, that I might make merry with my friends. But as soon as this son of yours came, who has devoured your livelihood with harlots, you killed the fatted calf for him.'" (Luke 15:29–30)

I didn't know about this conversation until the following day. I was still thinking about the service and the love and kindness shown to me that morning. In fact, after the meal I had suggested that the five of us have a little Communion service, to ask God's blessing on our family at this new beginning. I was surprised when Irene and Don rejected the idea. They left soon afterward.

I was confused about Irene's reaction the entire weekend. For years she had insisted that she wanted nothing more than for us to be close and that my disobedience and rebellion prevented all that. During my months at the shelter, I thought how Irene of all people would rejoice at my change, at my new commitment. It didn't make sense to me that she seemed even more hostile than ever. Don too seemed to want to avoid speaking with me. Shouldn't a pastor, of all people, want to celebrate when a sinner repents? But then I recalled that once Irene had called me an "easy repenter." Is that what she thought I was doing now?

I learned from Mother days later that Irene had told her some shocking news. During her brief visit to Allentown, she visited her best friend, Jean Brobst, who lived in neighboring Emmaus. They had been friends since attending the Mennonite Sunday school decades earlier. As they visited together that afternoon, Jean happened to mention about the couple whose back garden adjoined theirs. They had just adopted a baby girl. Irene immediately asked when that was. "Oh, it was the first week of this month, I believe," Jean said.

"What sort of people are they?" Irene wanted to know, trying to stay calm.

"They go to the Lutheran Church," Jean said.

"What's the wife like?" Irene asked.

"Oh, Betty is a nurse . . . with red hair . . ."

"What's the little girl's name?" Irene could barely ask.

"Susan Joseph."

So Irene returned to our home and announced to our mother that she learned where my baby was placed and that her name was now Susan Joseph. It was quite a shock to learn that, but I sensed that God had some reason for allowing me to have this slender link with my daughter.

CHAPTER TEN

When I was a child of seven and the Weiss Sisters sang regularly in conferences and services throughout the area, we met a family from near Reading called the Schwenks. The parents and their two grown daughters also traveled and sang in a variety of churches, and their younger daughter, Ruth, in addition played the trumpet, marimba, and xylophone. Ruth was almost fifteen years older than I, very tall and handsome, with an arresting personality that made a great impression on this young child. She was already active in Youth for Christ work throughout Pennsylvania, and Child Evangelism, and when a decade later young Billy Graham first made an appearance in the Philadelphia area, she was on the platform with him. She wore striking clothes, with large hats and voluminous fur coats, and I thought she must be terribly rich. Even so, she'd bend down and take time to speak to me affectionately.

Our families continued to meet as years passed. We considered the Schwenks close friends. I learned in later years that not only was Ruth a well-known Christian singer and evangelist in the area, she was a successful businesswoman, and later became co-owner of a local mining company. She seemed to be someone who made a success of everything she touched.

That summer of 1955, at the start of my new life, Ruth unexpectedly appeared at our door one day. Although I had not shared my secret experience with anyone outside the family, my mother thought it would be right to speak with Ruth, who would give me good advice. I was surprised when Ruth suggested I spend a few days with her in her home. I was quick to accept the offer. I could use some guidance in planning the next phase of my journey.

Ruth became a priceless friend and mentor during those days. She had a way of listening to any confession without criticizing or condemning. She was simply the most loving and kind woman I had ever met.

Ruth was now almost forty, unmarried, still active in an assortment of Christian ventures, balancing these with her secular career. But her focus was always on her love for the Lord's work. Everything else was secondary. Some might think it was a magnetic personality that defined her, but even then I sensed it was very much more than that.

Ruth encouraged me to return to college and finish what I had started. I would now be several years older than others in my year, but it was essential that I prepare myself adequately for whatever God wanted to do in me. By the time I returned to Allentown several days later, I had made a firm decision. I felt I had taken the next step in my Christian life.

I applied to King's College, New York, the Christian college Irene and Don graduated from a few years earlier, and was accepted as a second-year student. I was also welcomed back as a summer employee at Sears Roebuck which helped me to save a small amount toward the coming year's fees.

Soon after my visit with Ruth Schwenk, I decided I would like to be rebaptized. I thought of that old photo of myself at age seven, in a wet bathing suit, stumbling from the waters of baptism. Our pastor at that time, Rev. Musselman, had just released me after baptizing me in Allentown's Jordan River. I had asked to be baptized without any pressure from my parents. This was a few years after going to the altar at age five to "ask Jesus into my heart."

But that summer of 1955 I wanted to put the old life well and truly behind me, to be symbolically cleansed of all the sin, rebellion, disobedience, and denial of my Lord that had taken place in the intervening years. I was more convinced with each succeeding month that I was already a "new creature in Christ." I profoundly believed that the real cleansing had already been done. That feeble cry of mine, on March 15, 1955, in the Salvation Army was only the beginning. Over the next few months I became reacquainted with the Word of God, absorbing sermons and worshiping the Lord through the words of familiar hymns and restored relationships with the good people of Bethel Church. I felt like a heavenly delete button had been pressed and all those dark years had been wiped out. "Old things have passed away; behold, all things have become new" (2 Cor. 5:17).

The appropriately named Jordan River that was used in past years to baptize many Mennonites was no longer available. A swimming pool belonging to a church member was used instead. I recall that sunny day, coming up from the pool, my white sundress clinging to my body as family and friends sang some of the old hymns and choruses that presented me with new meaning.

You ask me why I'm happy,
Well, I'll just tell you why,
Because my sins are gone!
And when I meet the scoffers who ask me where they are
I say, "My sins are gone!"

They're underneath the blood on the cross of Calvary,
As far removed as darkness is from dawn;

In the sea of God's forgetfulness, that's good enough
   for me,
Praise God, my sins are gone!

from "My Sins Are Gone" by N. B. Vandall (1936)

Irene and I learned to sing that song when I was just a child of five, but it never meant as much to me then as it did now. Yes, sometimes the memory of this event or that relationship would suddenly appear before me, but I knew that that life was over; it did not tempt me again. I was just thankful that my parents never knew the full story of their prodigal daughter.

That summer I witnessed for the first time a Plymouth Brethren group of believers which showed me quite a different manifestation of the Christian church. Their services were so informal that nothing was planned ahead of time. One man might stand and give a prayer; another would give a Bible reading. Then one would suggest a hymn to be sung. And another brother would feel directed to share a word from the Lord. It could last ten minutes or thirty. I marveled at how the obvious spontaneity fused into a meaningful theme. I was reminded that it was simply the Holy Spirit at work. There was a holy atmosphere present that was quite different from that of any of the other churches I had visited, and it seemed fresh and powerful compared to the Mennonite routines with which I was familiar. It appealed to me very much.

That autumn I entered King's College, Briarcliff Manor, New York, and was once again a college student, but this time I loved every minute of the classes, my studies, the Christian environment, and my classmates. I had never been this conscientious with learning before, and I was having the time of my life. I had a room to myself—a world away from that grim attic room at the Salvation Army—and I took new pride in furnishing it and keeping it neat. I was particularly thankful for the work that I found. I was now a secretary in the public relations office from noon to five, five days a week, I babysat for a local dentist and his wife regularly, and later on I became a weekend nanny to twin girls in their beautiful home. God was meeting all my needs, and each week I put my earnings in the top dresser drawer to be ready for my monthly payment of one hundred dollars due at the end of each month. I was grateful that I didn't have to ask my parents for anything; they had already done so much for me!

And at the end of every month, the one hundred dollars was there ready for me to take to the bursar. One day, a few days before my payment was due, I received a letter from Jane, my Salvation Army friend. And out of the envelope tumbled two dollar bills. I was shocked, and moved. I said: "Lord! Why did You let her do that? I had my payment ready to take without it!" I was well aware that Jane's stipend from the Army was a lowly twenty-six dollars a month, so that represented a sizable gift from her. But when I went to the top drawer and counted out the money I'd saved, it came to just ninety-eight dollars. It was a precious lesson that God would meet *all* my needs, even when I didn't think it necessary!

I continued to treasure this new life, new forgiveness, new hope that Jesus supplied. I was a few years older physically than the girls in my dorm, but sometimes I felt decades older in experience. Yet I did not envy their innocent lives. I realized that although my sins grieved the Savior most of all, and certainly my parents, and still taunted me with sudden reminders, I was beginning to appreciate for the first time how special my life was. I began to be thankful that I was who I was. God had accepted me and planned a wonderful future for me. I was content!

Often, returning from my babysitting job in the village, I'd pass a lovely old stone-built church on the corner, called All Saints Episcopal Church. I was fascinated with the beauty of the tiny building and suddenly felt drawn to see what a service was like. The following Sunday I arrived in time for the Holy Eucharist. It was the most formal liturgy I'd ever seen, and yet I was captivated by the beautiful prayers which I repeated and meant with all my heart. There may have been some there who had not experienced the forgiveness and mercy of Christ that I had, and just said the prayers as a weekly routine. But I could have wept as the words went deep into my spirit.

Before the service ended, the rector gave some announcements and invited anyone who would like to lead a teenage Sunday school class to see him after church. I didn't have to think twice; I knew this was what God wanted me to do! I hurried forward after the benediction and offered my help. I told him I was a student at King's, was studying the Bible, and would love to take the class. I walked out of my first Episcopal service as their brand-new Sunday school teacher!

Those Sunday classes were a joy to us all. The young boys and girls were not used to studying why Jesus had to die and how to be a true follower of Him. Now each one was eager to learn more. When I suggested a parents' night so that we could let their families know what they were learning, they agreed eagerly. The night the parents came we all looked at Ephesians 1 and Paul's prayer to "all saints." I was full of thanksgiving to God for this challenging opportunity He had given me.

I wrote all about my new class to my parents and described the great responses of the teenagers and of their families as well. I knew it would bless them to hear of it. I wasn't prepared for a letter that arrived from my brother-in-law, Don, who chastised me for even attending the Episcopal church and then getting involved in the working of it. He wrote: "Come out from among them and be separate, . . . do not touch what is unclean" (2 Cor. 6:17). He warned me that we can have no fellowship with unbelievers any more than light can have fellowship with darkness. I was shocked that he would condemn my first form of Christian service! Of course he was now a Baptist minister and I was brand-new to evangelistic ministry. But how could God tell me one thing and Don another? I was baffled.

CHAPTER ELEVEN

In the following year, I continued to attend the Episcopal church and teach the class. I also attended Sunday evening meetings at the nearby Plymouth Brethren group. I was getting a well-rounded education of the Christian church, with all the various emphases and taboos.

One day in November my mother rang me with exciting news. Two single, elderly sisters from the Mennonite church had asked if I might agree to meet a young British scientist who had recently arrived in the country and had taken rooms in the house adjoining theirs. I was returning home for the Thanksgiving holidays, and he asked to meet me the next weekend if I were willing. I knew little about him except that his name was Dr. Tony Holland and that he had just begun work at Air Products Chemicals in Allentown.

I had little success in the dating department in the few years of my studies at King's College. Since I was older than my classmates, of the few young men in the senior class that took my fancy, all were spoken for. My time at King's thus far had been blissfully happy, with good companions in the women's dorm, great classes and professors, and interesting chapel speakers that helped enlarge our vision of the worldwide ministries available to graduates. I began thinking it unlikely that I would find a husband at King's or anywhere, with such a checkered past. And as I explored the Christian opportunities opening up all over the world, I suspected that perhaps I would remain single. This didn't fill me with dread; I often recalled the words of the psalm that promised "fullness of joy" to those who lived in God's presence (Ps. 16:11). My future was in the hands of a loving Lord.

This offer of a blind date with a young Englishman took me by surprise. I had hopeful visions of a handsome Prince Philip greeting me with a charming accent to match. I accepted the invitation and looked forward to meeting this dashing stranger. The evening of our date, a jovial bespectacled man crossed the threshold of our home and could not have been more chivalrous. He might not look like Prince Philip, and he appeared more bookish than dashing, but he was lovely all the same. He quoted Shakespeare to me and treated me with more respect and interest than any date had ever done. He had already learned that I sang regularly in church and now asked me to sing for him. I chose, "I Would Love to Tell You What I Think of Jesus." I got the impression after that that he was smitten. He invited me to dinner and a concert in Philadelphia for the following night.

Never before had I been taken to such a beautiful restaurant, after which Tony bought me a large box of chocolates, and then we sat back in good seats to watch Eugene Ormandy directing the Philadelphia Philharmonic Orchestra, on one of the most memorable evenings of my life thus far.

During the meal, and after the concert, Tony told me about himself and how he had arrived in the USA from his home in Cheshire. He had won scholarships to Durham, then Oxford, then London universities, first studying physics and later moving into chemical engineering. He spent several years in British industry after obtaining his PhD degree at the age of twenty-six. At the age of thirty, he noticed an ad for British scientists and engineers to emigrate to the USA. It was the season of the "brain drain" when companies in the USA saw the advantage of recruiting those with British graduate degrees to work for them. Tony felt it would be helpful to have a few years' experience in American industry. Upon arrival at the American embassy, he was offered a position with Air Products then and there. Their headquarters was situated in Allentown, Pennsylvania, my hometown.

During the course of the evening and our conversations, I told him that I was a committed Christian, and he assured me that he was one too. He struck me as a very clean-living, responsible man, with no taint of a wild side in him. He didn't have that flashy look of my former suitors, that flirtatious and even menacing manner that appealed to me in former years. Frankly, he looked more old-fashioned than I expected, with out-of-date glasses and a slightly unfashionable suit and raincoat. But what he lacked in fashion, he more than made up for it in courtesy and kindness.

It was an eventful weekend, as Tony wanted to see me every night. And when I was getting ready to return to New York, he offered to drive me for the hundred mile trip. I knew I was being rushed, and this was a bit worrying, because I was not absolutely certain that he was a believer as I was. Many good people imagine themselves to be Christian without taking that critical step of full trust in Christ. My mother's church friends, the Lerch sisters, had described him as a true English gentleman, even though, they said, he was not a believer. I did not intend to get involved with anyone that was not a real Christian. The night he drove me from Allentown to my college in New York, I asked him about miracles. "As a scientist, do you believe in miracles? The virgin birth, for example?"

Tony looked surprised. "Of course I do! Look, science is only the description of God's handiwork!" and I breathed a sigh of relief. I wondered why the Lerch sisters doubted his salvation.

I phoned and asked them about it a few days later. "Why, he smokes a *pipe!*" they replied. Ah, the good old Mennonite yardstick for determining one's relationship to Christ!

Having solved that problem, I allowed Tony to pick me up at the start of the Christmas holidays some weeks later. I could not deny that I was flattered that such a brilliant and courteous man was interested in me, but I was unsure whether I wanted this. After all, he was hardly the "dream man" that I had envisioned all those years. (Not that *that* dream had served me at all well.)

The day college classes closed for the holidays, the students were all milling about in the large common room at the front of the administration building. Tony had gone up to my room to help with my luggage, and we came down into the common room together—I with one suitcase, and Tony struggling with the two largest ones. As we crossed the center of the room, it seemed that all talking ceased. The disadvantage with King's was the small student body, where everyone knew everyone else's business. Outsiders were scrutinized and often felt unwelcome. But all I felt at that moment was embarrassment and shame as the cluster of guys over by the mailbox stopped and stared at my slightly balding and unfashionable suitor. As we neared the door, Tony struggled to open it while trying to balance the cases.

The guys lounging near the mailboxes kept staring and didn't move a muscle.

We finally made it out the door, with difficulty, and once on the other side, Tony turned his face to me. He was red-faced and very angry. "I have never seen such rudeness in all my life!" he fumed. "It was intolerable for them to stand there refusing to help a stranger who was trying to open the door!"

And that was the turning point for me. Moments before, I had selfishly felt shame that my macho classmates would see me with an older man. But I should have felt shame that they so rudely ignored a stranger's needs. Tony had every right to be angry. They had no right to stare at him and refuse to help. In that moment I knew it was time to revise my "dream man." And I looked at Tony with new eyes.

Now released from the shackles of public opinion, I welcomed Tony visiting me at King's every weekend. I saw more clearly with each visit that he was an exceptional man and a particularly devout Christian. He had been raised in a nominal Christian home and attended Methodist Sunday schools when young. But at grammar school, he absorbed teaching that the Bible was "unscientific" and outdated. By the time he went to university, he considered himself an agnostic. But at the age of thirty, when working in London, he went to a Methodist hall one night and heard a sermon on the apostle Paul and his Damascus Road experience. The speaker was Rev. Fletcher-Fleet, and the sermon challenged Tony and gripped his heart. When he went back to his rooms, he wondered, *Could there be a personal God? Might He care for me? Does He wish to communicate with us? What role does Jesus play in this plan?*

Over the course of the next weeks and months, Tony came to experience his own Damascus Road miracle, and he, too, became "a new creation" "in Christ" (2 Cor. 5:17). Only a few months later he answered the ad for British engineers to work in America.

As we spent more and more time together, it was obvious that Tony loved me. He began to talk about his life in England, and his intention to move back there. Finally he asked, "Do you think you would like to go?" I said, "I would love to!"

As a student of English literature, I often pictured myself in the places where the writers and poets of Britain lived.

"No, I mean, permanently. To marry me." There. He'd come out with it!

But I knew a difficult confession had to come first. I couldn't agree to anything until I told him about the baby that I'd given away and the years of prodigal living before that. Would he be quite so eager to marry me after he heard my story? I knew he had already put me on a pedestal that I did not deserve. If that came tumbling down, would it change his mind?

We sat in the car that night, with the lights out, and I told him about my years-long fight with my parents, church, and God—the bad choices, the deceit. And finally the child I gave up for adoption.

There was a stunned silence in the car for some moments. I didn't dare look at him. Finally, he said, "If Jesus forgave you, I can do no less."

Wedding, May 1958

TONY

Copperfield sketch, 1980

The Holland family at Copperfield, 1966-87

We were married in a small ceremony in the Mennonite church in Allentown, in May 1958, with only thirty of my relatives in attendance, plus Misses Anna and Lillian Lerch, the heroines of the day who had played cupid for the happy couple. Tony was still rather shy in American social settings, and he was relieved that I was willing to forgo a large wedding. Tony's mother planned to come over for a lengthy visit after our week-long honeymoon in Canada.

I completed my final year toward my BA as Mrs. Holland, then I began work at Prentice-Hall Publishers as a book writer and took night courses at New York University toward an MA in British and American literature. Meanwhile Tony was offered a job with Lever Brothers and eventually became process development manager. During his time there, he was responsible for developing the DEFI process that would become Lever's greatest asset: DOVE bars. Thereafter I proudly thought of my husband as "Dr. Dove!" It was during this time that he began to write for technical journals and later published textbooks that proved to be quite successful in the years to come.

But during one interview for a newspaper, a journalist asked him what his proudest achievement was. He promptly replied: "Accepting Jesus Christ as my Lord and Savior," which rendered the journalist speechless. During our time living and working in the New York area, we profited greatly from our involvement with Grace Chapel, a Brethren assembly. Tony, particularly, gained valuable Bible teaching which he did not have in his early years. He also decided to request adult baptism.

My parents were not exactly happy that we planned to move to England in the future, but they greatly respected Tony and the four of us were very close. Irene often fretted, reminding me that our plans to return to England would "break up the family." Irene and Don had by this time adopted two beautiful children, and some years later I gave birth to Christopher and Jonathan. Irene mourned the fact that I was depriving her children from getting to know their cousins as they all grew up.

However, on numerous occasions when Tony and I asked to go down to Pennsylvania to visit them, Irene had various reasons why it was not convenient. Sometimes she'd say, "If only you could have come last weekend," or "It would have suited me if you could have come next weekend." I could not put my finger on the problem, but it seemed to me that despite her protests of wanting to keep the family together, all too often she did not seem eager to see us.

I was well aware of her great disappointment: that she was unable to bear children. I had assumed, incorrectly, that when she adopted Donald and Susan, that disappointment would be lifted. But as beautiful as those children were, she admitted that she found it a bitter experience each time one of her friends gave birth. She could not rejoice with them as they expected. She dreaded baby showers. I hoped that in time she would get over this.

During the summer of 1964, we were living in New Jersey, in an apartment block on the cliffs overlooking Manhattan. We had a patch of grass in front of our ground floor apartment which was an ideal space to entertain visitors when the weather was fine. That was the summer we arranged to have a party of friends from International Students (ISI), a Christian organization that encouraged Christian families to welcome foreign students into their homes. Tony and I had regularly entertained Indian doctors, African businessmen, a Vietnamese banker, Panamanian students, and others. We decided to have a lawn party to welcome them all together. In their midst, seven-month-old Christopher enjoyed people-watching from his playpen surrounded by those colorfully attired visitors.

I was putting out the dishes of food when the doorbell rang. To my amazement, there stood Irene and Don and children. What a surprise! I was glad to see them, and fortunately there was plenty of food to go around, but I thought at that moment, *I wouldn't dare do that to her!* She would not welcome me coming without warning! I realized then that there was one rule for Irene and another for me.

🍂 CHAPTER THIRTEEN

In the next few years, as Tony's writing for technical journals increased, he began to consider the possibility of applying for academic posts in England. He realized that he was able to describe technical problems in a direct, concise way that appealed to publishers and to the students who read the journals. He often found other writers' technical articles and textbooks unnecessarily cumbersome and sought to describe subjects in his own field as simply as possible. He began to feel he might do well in academic life; he thought his background in British and American industry would equip him well to teach chemical engineering subjects in the same particular way that he had begun to write of them.

In 1965, Tony learned of an opening for a chemical engineering professor and head of department at the newly formed University of Salford, Manchester. After we talked and prayed about it, he applied for the post. It was the closest university to his home village in Cheshire where his widowed mother still lived. It would be an ideal situation to live and work within a short distance of her home.

The following year there were three major changes in the family. Tony flew to England to candidate for the chair at Salford and was offered the professorship. Our second son, Jonathan, was born that spring. And my beloved Daddy was found to have advanced cancer. Even as we celebrated Tony's new appointment and the birth of our son, we were torn with the news of Daddy's declining health. It was particularly hard for me, because we planned to move to England that summer so that Tony could take up his post at Salford in August.

Daddy was only sixty-six, but that gentle uncomplaining spirit that blessed so many lives did not change in his remaining months. He may have been sorry to leave his family, but he never uttered a word of complaint. His lifetime of complete devotion to his Lord Jesus Christ meant that whatever happened in his life, he took all with equanimity. When at one time he suddenly lost his job, he announced it calmly, knowing God would provide. During the turmoil of my teen years, he never once raised his voice, but I learned later that many tears were shed in his bedroom as he fasted and prayed for me there.

This gentle Christian was loved by most people, but at work one man in particular hated him for his quiet and consistent witness. John D. would often walk past Daddy's workbench and toss in a swear word or an off-color joke, hoping to upset him. But Daddy did not upset easily and always replied to John's comments lovingly and patiently. After a few years of this, John became curious about Daddy's faith and accepted an invitation to our church. In time John had his own "Damascus Road experience" in the Mennonite church on North Eighth Street. John became a greatly loved elder in the church for the rest of his life.

Even as I saw Daddy getting weaker, I thanked the Lord that I had committed my life to Christ when I did, and that Daddy and I had been able to enjoy a loving bond for eleven years. I thanked God that Daddy had witnessed my marriage to a fine Christian and had seen our two little sons. I regretted that he would not now be able to visit me in England, where we

VICKI HARLEY HOLLAND

planned to settle in a few months. I knew I would mourn that
wonderful man for the rest of my life.

That summer of 1966 even as I was learning to let go of
Daddy, I was looking forward to a totally new era in the life of
our young family. During those months we began preparations
to sell or give away our life of the past nine years. Since our marriage began, we had kept ourselves surprisingly mobile, living in
a two-room apartment for most of that time. Only in the previous two years had we allowed ourselves one additional room as
the babies arrived. No TV or new car for us, despite the rampant
consumerism that surrounded us. That summer we were ready
to renounce our meager possessions and sell or give away all our
furniture, retaining only our clothing, a set of silverware, and an
oriental carpet to take with us for our new life in England.

We surrendered our nine-year-old Ford on the final day—a
friend gave us one hundred dollars for it. It had served us well
even when many of our friends had traded their cars three or
four times during the lifetime of our standard model Ford. We
had kept to our promise to keep free of entanglements as our
eyes were fixed on a future in England, a future that would be
easier to slip into if we were unencumbered with the trappings
of the "American Dream."

Two-year-old Christopher watched as day by day friends came
to pick up a sofa here, a bookcase there, pictures, mirrors, and finally tables and chairs. On the last night the apartment was almost
bare save for our bed, a crib, and the carriage where two-month-
old Jonathan slept. Those would be carried off in the morning by a
Panamanian couple. Our exodus worked like a military campaign.

In the midst of all this upheaval on one of the last days, we
welcomed a special visitor into our home: Major Ian Thomas,
British evangelist that was bringing a Deeper Life message to
the USA that year. In many churches and auditoriums he shared

his message: "Christ Who Is Our Life." My mother had been greatly impressed with his ministry, even entertaining him in her home during his speaking schedule in Pennsylvania. I too had read his book and was gripped by his message—although it would be some years before Tony and I more fully understood and embraced his teaching with all our hearts.

Nevertheless when we learned he was speaking in the New York area, we drove across the river to hear him. After the meeting I found myself inviting him to dine with us the following day. Despite the absence of the usual complement of tables and chairs, with the minimum of decorations, he seemed oblivious to the barren surroundings and was clearly more in tune with the life of Christ within. We never forgot his prayer as we stood together in that half-empty dining room in North Bergen, New Jersey. He dedicated us into the Lord's keeping and specifically thanked God for the home in England that God had already chosen for us. Major Thomas's earnest prayer blessed us and remained with us for years to come. God indeed had chosen the perfect home for us, which we found just eleven days after our arrival in Manchester that July.

Our little family said good-bye to our American home and family, and we sizzled in the heat of a New York air terminal registering ninety-four degrees that night. Seven hours later we arrived into a cloudy, cool Manchester morning of fifty-four degrees. I told Tony, "The whole country is air-conditioned!"

The moment I saw a beautiful ivy-covered, double-gabled brick home in Altrincham called "Copperfield" it was love at first sight. But it took a few more months to renovate it to our specifications. During the building work, Tony traveled to Salford to begin his new position, driving from his mother's home in South Cheshire each day. It was a long journey of almost two hours each way. We were grateful for Mother Holland's loving and patient care and her offer for us to remain with her as long as necessary. Her gentle spirit was very much like my Daddy's. She bore any problem with dignity and grace and never seemed to get flustered, even with a lively two-year-old now running throughout her small house and garden and a baby often crying at inappropriate times. She was always a perfect mother-in-law.

In November we finally moved into Copperfield, which had generous gardens front and rear. My new furniture was delivered during the next few days but our celebration was marred by the news of my Daddy's death on November 17. We had decided that I would not return for the funeral which we knew would take place within a few months after flying to England. I knew beyond any doubt that my Daddy was now with the Lord he served so faithfully all his life.

Even as Tony was settling down to his new university responsibilities, we looked for a local church where we could worship as a family. We had enjoyed nine years of fellowship with the Plymouth Brethren community in the USA and now found a small similar chapel near our home. But it didn't have any children's facilities and I often found myself hastily leaving the service when one or both of the boys began to fret or talk. The Brethren valued silence and noisy children were not in evidence there. After some months we began attending a nearby Baptist church which catered to all ages—including babies and children. It gave young mothers the opportunity to enjoy a quiet Sunday service without interruption.

By the end of my first year living in England, I considered it as natural and normal to me as breathing. I loved every minute of my new life, watching our little sons growing there, enjoying my beautiful home, entertaining other couples from church or the university. Tony's work at the university gave him much pleasure, and of course, he was happy to be back in his home country after nine years abroad.

That first year we were surprised and thrilled to receive an invitation to one of the Buckingham Palace's summer Garden Parties. Tony was chosen to represent the university as their youngest professor. But I could scarcely imagine my good fortune as guards waved us through the gates of the palace to the vast gardens at the back. We took our places at tiny tables on the palace lawn where we were served strawberries and cream and tea while two bands played at opposite ends of the gardens overlooking the flamingo-filled lake. The Queen, Prince Philip, and other members of the Royal Family mingled with guests, although their own "tea" was taken in a special tent on the other side of the lawn. During the festivities, Tony leaned over and teased me. "Well, Vera Weiss of Liberty Street, what do you think of all this?"

I was not at all aware of a "leanness of soul" creeping into my life during those happy years. I enjoyed our many Christian friends, services, and conferences we occasionally attended. We hosted a special New Year's Eve dinner party each year for a dozen Christian couples, always one of the highlights of our year. I felt my life was complete and I was never homesick for my life in America.

Then, suddenly, in 1970, I felt a strong urge to return to the USA. I had not been back for four years, and I thought it was time to visit my mother in Pennsylvania and Irene's family who now lived in Buffalo, New York. Christopher would stay at home and continue his studies at Altrincham Prep School but Jonathan was only four and therefore free to accompany me to the States. Anyway, he loved stories of cowboys and Indians and was longing to see real Indians whooping across the prairies just like those he saw on television. I could not guarantee that he would be successful.

CHAPTER FOURTEEN

It was good to be with my mother again, although she looked sad and lonely without Daddy. Her hearing had got progressively worse and Daddy had always patiently repeated the many comments and conversations she missed. Now there was no one to take his place. Mother and I talked almost nonstop the first few days about all the changes that had occurred locally and nationally in my absence. Finally I mentioned that I needed to phone Irene to arrange to take the bus to see her. Mother suddenly looked troubled.

"What's wrong?" I asked.

"Well, she's still upset . . ." she said quietly.

"Upset? About me? Why on earth would she be upset?"

"You know . . . the baby . . ."

I was furious. I had given birth in 1955, fifteen years earlier. Through that, I had discovered new life in Christ and never looked back. I had married a fine Christian man, obtained two degrees and bore two sons. I was living for the Lord. What more did she want of me?

I went up to my room, trembling with anger. I sat there for a long while, nursing my wounds. Finally I picked up my Bible and opened it. It seemed to open at the first chapter of John's first epistle: "If we say that we have fellowship with Him, and walk in darkness, we lie and do not practice the truth. But if we walk in the light, as He is in the light, we have fellowship with one another, and the blood of Jesus Christ His Son cleanses us from all sin" (vv. 6–7).

I read those verses over and over, and for the first time in a very long while I saw something new and disturbing in them. I'd memorized that entire chapter as a child and could still recall every verse. But did I really *know* what John was saying?

I did not have fellowship with my own sister. That was the first discovery. So how could I be walking in the light? I would have protested only an hour earlier that I was in and of the Light. But suddenly there was an illumination like an X ray of my soul that revealed a bitterness in me! My first reaction had been to give up on Irene. Okay, if she didn't want to see me, fine. It would save me the trouble and money of going up there. I didn't need this constant disapproval from her!

But the more I looked at those verses, the more I knew I had to "walk in the light."

I started down the stairs ready to tell Mother of my discovery. Suddenly I sank down on the last step, and a powerful picture or vision rose before me, of a steamroller running over me, crumbling me to pieces. I thought of the cryptic words of the prophets quoted by Jesus before His crucifixion: "Whoever falls on this stone will be broken; but on whomever it falls, it will grind him to powder." I knew I had fallen on the Lord Jesus all those years ago, and He had broken me of my defiance and rebellion. But now once again I recognized the work of God in crushing something else out of me. I stood up, and that "steamroller" had in seconds crushed all the anger and resentment out of me! I was immediately overwhelmed with the light and love of Jesus, more than I had felt in years.

In those moments there came a remarkable change in me.

Not only was I now eager to see Irene, I was now aware of my own self-righteousness. I had judged her severely; I had not even thought to judge myself. But as I became more aware of my own hypocrisy, I became more fully aware of the power of the Holy Spirit within me. In fact it was simply His presence that was revealing the corners of darkness in my soul. Why had I not seen this before?

I was beginning to see that my public Christian face was not always what God saw in me. I had been thoroughly satisfied with my comfortable Christian existence in England. Now I was aware of the pride that had crept into me—pride and bitterness and unforgiveness. I had for years led a Bible study at Copperfield every Tuesday morning. Women from a variety of denominations, including Catholic, loved to come and listen to what I prepared. My Mennonite background afforded me a wealth of sermons and studies and memorized passages to assist me. Now suddenly I knew I had been living on spiritual capital for a long time, but was I walking "in the light as He is in the light"? All of this came over me in a flash as I was sitting on the bottom step in my mother's small dining room.

After telling my mother what happened to me, I phoned Irene and told her I wanted to come and to bring Jonathan to see her. She finally agreed. Mother was relieved.

The day before we left for Buffalo, Ruth Schwenk turned up for an unexpected visit. She always seemed to surface at the right time for me! It had been fifteen years since we last met, and we might have spent hours catching up on family news and gossip, but all I wanted to relate to her was how the Holy Spirit steamrolled over me as I sat on the stair. Ruth laughed joyously and told me that she had something to report to me too. She related how, in the perfect timing of God, she had lost her business and had taken ill. As she was set aside for a time, she began to question the direction of her life and whether in fact she was doing all that God wanted her to do. And that's when she felt He was saying to her, *It's not what I want you to do, Ruth; it's what I want you to* be. *I want you to be in Me and I in you. Just live in Me. That's all I want.* She discovered through that powerful inner voice that she had been ceaselessly *working for* the Lord, where He only wanted her to *rest in* Him. That was the day Ruth, the evangelical singer, musician, preacher, and organizer, left everything to follow *Him*.

She had been heading for an evangelical burnout, overworking for the Lord. But He did not want her to be a Martha; He wanted her to be a Mary. "Martha, Martha, you are worried and troubled about many things. But one thing is needed, and Mary has chosen that good part, which will not be taken away from her" (Luke 10:41–42).

I knew as surely as I breathed that God had planned for me to return to the USA to deal with my pride, to meet and forgive Irene, to comfort my mother, and to meet Ruth again and learn from her.

The visit to Buffalo was a success on several levels. The family adored Jonathan and his British accent. Furthermore, Irene did something for me that I will never forget. She arranged for Jonathan to meet an eighty-two-year-old Indian chief, the Grand Sachem of the Sand Turtle clan of the Tuscarora Indians that lived on the Iroquois reservation near Buffalo. Chief Green was a Christian believer and pastor and was delighted to welcome into his home the little Englishman who was wearing a Woolworth headdress and had a plastic tomahawk clutched in his hand. And when Chief Green, splendid in a real eagle-feathered headdress, sat on a stool beside his potbellied stove in his front room and began to chant softly, Jonathan hopped and whooped, dancing in a circle around the old chief, having the time of his life.

But of far greater importance, the whole incident brought revival to my soul. Often God can only use crises to get our attention. My self-justification was not one whit better than anything my sister did or felt. God used that incident to take me out of the darkness of my complacency. Irene never knew what a precious gift she gave me that year.

CHAPTER FIFTEEN

On my return to England, a vicar friend of ours asked me out of the blue, "What happened to you? Whatever it was, will you tell me about it? How can I get it?" I could only say that I had had a powerful encounter with the Holy Spirit and felt a new and overwhelming love for Jesus.

I realized this had happened as a result of repenting of my pride and resentment toward Irene. And although she and I had not had the frank talk I had hoped for, I knew in my heart that I had "come clean" to God about my unloving feelings. I could only hope and pray that at some time in the future, Irene might be willing to do the same.

In the months to come, I began to wonder whether all the events that kept me busy "for the Lord" were as worthwhile as I had formerly thought. I recalled Ruth's frantic rush to keep busy for God and her sudden awareness that He wanted her to simply abide in Him and allow the Lord Jesus to take fuller control of her life. I began seeing that not all one's Christian activities were achieving what I'd hoped they would achieve. Was I running ahead of God? Should I be waiting and listening more?

I began to rise earlier each morning and tiptoe down to the morning room to read the Bible and pray for an hour or more before the others stirred. I found a new peace to deal with whatever unexpected events occurred during the days. I was more conscious than ever of living *in Christ*. Although it was difficult explaining this, I did not feel it necessary to talk about my "experience." I did however seem to have a new freedom to talk about the presence and power of the Holy Spirit in a believer's life.

I longed to meet up with Ruth again and gain more of her insights. I felt she and I were traveling the same road, but she was far ahead of me. One day I wrote to her and asked, *Could you possibly come and visit us? And stay for as long as you like?*

Two days later I was amazed to see an envelope from her pushed through my postbox. That was quick! But when I opened the letter, I was even more surprised. It had been dated a full week before, even days before I'd written to her. She wrote, *I believe the Lord is urging me to come and visit you. May I? When would it be convenient?*

For six weeks I enjoyed wonderful fellowship and teaching with my beloved Ruth. I was able to see the importance of stripping away all of the excess of duties and meetings and conferences and just wait on the Lord. I felt that God was teaching me a new way of resting in Him, of true worship, of sitting at the Master's feet and simply enjoying His presence. And, to my surprise, things began to happen more readily and effectively than ever before. Ruth referred me to an old poem by A. B. Simpson which so clearly summarized the revival experience we both shared.

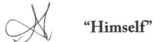 **"Himself"**

Once it was the blessing, now it is the Lord;
Once it was the feeling, now it is His Word.

Once His gifts I wanted, now the Giver own;
Once I sought for healing, now Himself alone.

Once 'twas painful trying, now 'tis perfect trust;
Once a half salvation, now the uttermost.
Once 'twas ceaseless holding, now He holds me fast;
Once 'twas constant drifting, now my anchor's cast.

Once 'twas busy planning, now 'tis trustful prayer;
Once 'twas anxious caring, now He has the care.
Once 'twas what I wanted, now what Jesus says;
Once 'twas constant asking, now 'tis ceaseless praise.

Once it was my working, His it hence shall be;
Once I tried to use Him, now He uses me.
Once the power I wanted, now the Mighty One;
Once for self I labored, now for Him alone.

Once I hoped in Jesus, now I know He's mine;
Once my lamps were dying, now they brightly shine.
Once for death I waited, now His coming hail;
And my hopes are anchored, safe within the veil.

Ever since the age of twelve, I had an uncontrollable terror of insects: spiders, daddy longlegs, roaches, cicadas, you name it. There were times that I ran screaming from the house if there was a large insect in the corner. I couldn't bear to look at it, but I couldn't bear to kill it either. I'd have to shut the door on it and avoid that room until Tony came home to deal with the dreaded thing. I recall one summer when we lived in New

Jersey, during a plague of cicadas, more commonly known as the seventeen-year locusts. They were everywhere, screaming in the trees, thousands of them, and I could hardly bear to walk to work beneath the wretched creatures. Once, in a park, a horde of them appeared above us in the trees. We had just set out a picnic with friends, but all I could think of was escaping the monsters, so I ran screaming to our car, flew into it, and rolled up the windows. Outside the temperature was 90 degrees, but despite the steaming heat within, I sat there, sobbing hysterically, unable to control my fear.

One of the things I looked forward to about moving to England was that I might escape the terrors of insects. Tony had told me that the summers were too cold for them to breed in Britain. He said even the mosquitoes didn't bite; the temperatures were too low for that. (He lied.) The American insects I most feared were the daddy longlegs, and Tony said they didn't exist in England. (Again he lied.) The first August after our move, I was horrified to note that not only were there British daddy longlegs, but they *flew*! In August they would come out of hiding and attach themselves to the windows, looking in at me! They made their homes in the hydrangea bushes outside our loggia and would fly up out of the bushes and land on the various windows where they enjoyed terrorizing me all day long.

One evening Tony and I went to a meeting nearby to hear a young Dutchman, Goos Vedder, who was a companion to Brother Andrew. They and others took Bibles into the Soviet Union at a time when it was extremely dangerous to do so. Goos was a wonderful young man—fearless and full of the Holy Spirit. I was deeply affected by his talk and after the meeting invited him to speak at our home the following night, when we had already planned a meeting for friends. He agreed.

Over twenty friends and neighbors were seated in our living room that evening as Goos shared a message from the text of 1 John 4:18: "Perfect love casts out fear." Even as he spoke, I recalled in recent days praying for more love for an individual who was giving me problems. The words he spoke went straight to my heart and I felt a surge of love rising within me. I knew God was touching my life in a special way.

The following morning I awoke and after my devotions walked out into our garden. Suddenly I went over to the hydrangea bushes and buried my hands deep within them. I knew I was healed! Twenty-five years of terror—a phobia no man could cure—were totally gone! I had not prayed to be rid of fear; I had prayed for more love. And the love drove out the fear. Don't ask me how to explain it: I cannot. But it happened, and from that moment on, I have never had a return of that phobia.

By 1975, Tony had taught for more than seven years at the university and was owed a sabbatical. It was not possible to accept a sabbatical position for an academic year as it would disturb the boys' work at their schools. But an opportunity arose for Tony to accept a summer's appointment at a chemical company in Pasadena, California. We decided that I could take the boys on ahead, fly to New York and then take a bus trip across the USA for them to see more of the country of their birth. We planned to stop and visit with friends and family scattered throughout the USA and stay with each for a night or two before resuming the trip. I had not been back home since Jonathan and I had visited in 1970. Christopher had left as a little boy of two, and now he was eleven. They were both excited at the prospect of this adventure.

I planned a schedule and then wrote letters to share my plans and ask if we might visit on given dates. Quickly we received answers from friends from New York to California: "Please come! Stay as long as you like!" But there was one exception. Irene replied that the date I'd given wasn't suitable. It was the night before her seventeen-year-old son was due to leave for camp, she replied, and she had to pack his clothing!

Once again I thought of the many times in previous years that it had not been "suitable" for us to visit. But this was particularly bizarre, since we had not seen each other for five years and she was refusing our visit so that she could pack her seventeen-year-old son's suitcase! I had to keep in mind my resolve of five years earlier to leave it all in God's hands. But as the Greyhound bus drove the three of us through Buffalo onto our next planned stop, I felt very sad that we still had not gotten to the bottom of her animosity.

The rest of our cross-country trip was a delight, and we were glad to meet Tony when we got off the bus in Los Angeles. He had flown in earlier in the week to rent an apartment for us. The months in California were a golden time for us all. In the final week, I learned of a Full Gospel Businessman's Fellowship (FGBMFI) convention in Anaheim in which Christian businessmen from around the world would speak and give accounts of how Jesus Christ had changed their lives.

Although God had brought revival to my soul in 1970 and I had come to live more simply in Jesus in the years since then, I had regretted that Tony seemed to distance himself from my experience. I wanted to share with him what it meant to just "abide in Christ." Although he accepted it intellectually, he was still a buttoned-up, introverted Englishman who did not let his emotions run away from him. He did not shirk from confessing that he was a Christian believer but he was careful to do it in a dignified British way!

I wanted in the worst way for us to go to Anaheim to experience the final night of the convention. Tony did not and begged to stay home. When he grudgingly drove us south on the freeway, and we got hopelessly lost, he decided that we were "meant" not to go and wanted to turn around. I believed with all my heart that it was important to carry on. We finally made it to the convention center.

That night it was Tony's turn to have a revelation. Eight thousand men and women had crowded into the hall for the final night, to hear men from a variety of Protestant and Catholic churches speak of the transforming power of Jesus in their lives and of the freedom and joy the Holy Spirit gives. My heart lifted to hear such testimonies, but I thought with sorrow that this was needed so desperately in secular Britain, where any independent Christian programming was forbidden on television.

On the flight back to England I thought of a verse I'd read recently that applied to this wonderful summer experience. Jesus said, "Go home to your friends and tell them what great things the Lord has done for you and how He has had compassion on you!" (Mark 5:19).

CHAPTER SIXTEEN

O n our return to the UK we learned that for several years there had been a small Full Gospel Businessmen's group meeting regularly in Preston, Lancashire. As soon as we were able we drove up to see what it was all about. Tony was blessed to enjoy the fellowship of Spirit-filled men and commented how much we needed such a group in our area. During the evening, we learned that the next FGBMFI convention was to be held in Miami on May 30. I longed for us to go there, but it seemed highly unlikely. I could not see how we could get away in less than a month, although I knew that with God nothing was impossible.

For weeks I waited anxiously for some sign that we might go to Miami. I knew we would have to be on the plane no later than May 29 in order to get there in time. It was beginning to look impossible.

The last week in May, I received a phone call from a woman in Droitwich, near Birmingham. She was a stranger to me, but she pointed out that she was a Christian and had heard of me from a friend. She asked if I might consider coming down to her area, to visit and minister there. She suggested I come for two weeks and she further said the Lord seemed to say I was to fast during that time! It made my head spin. Any unbeliever would think the woman was insane and perhaps that I too was insane to consider such a bizarre request. But something about it did not seem unreasonable, and God's ways are often not our ways. I put it to Tony when he came back from the university that evening, and surprisingly he agreed that it sounded right.

And so the following day, May 29, I was on the motorway heading to Birmingham. I had to laugh when I realized the date. I had longed to be flying to sunny Miami that day. But instead God put me on a bus to rainy Droitwich!

I was greeted lovingly by the young Christian couple and their two children. Sally was a nurse, and I felt comfortable allowing her to supervise the fast. As the days past, I suffered no hunger pains and after two days I began sitting with the family at the table during meals, with my glass of water, and it seemed perfectly natural to me. During the days, I had time to read and pray, and on occasions visited people with Sally and prayed with them. The first week went quickly.

On the eighth morning, I thought to myself, *This has been a good week, and I believe it was right that I came here, but perhaps one week is enough. Perhaps I could go back home now!* And then I picked up my Bible and turned to the passage for the day on a Bible reading chart that I was following. It was from the book of Ecclesiastes, and it read, "When you make a vow to God, do not delay to pay it; for He has no pleasure in fools. Pay what you have vowed—Better not to vow than to vow and not pay . . . nor say before the messenger of God that it was an error" (Eccl. 5:4–6).

I laughed aloud. Okay, okay! That settled it . . . I must remain another week! There was no doubt in my mind that for some reason this whole strange enterprise was part of God's plan.

The second week went just as well as the first, and I was able to exist comfortably on water, lemon juice, and weak tea with no ill effects. Of course I was relieved at the end of the two weeks, and on the final morning I began packing up my things to return home. But when I opened my Bible to that day's reading, I was shocked beyond words to read, "Paul implored them . . . saying, Today is the fourteenth day you have waited and continued without food, and eaten nothing. Therefore I urge you to take nourishment, for this is for your survival, since not a hair will fall from the head of any of you" (Acts 27:33–34).

When I returned home, I couldn't wait to tell Tony about the amazing verses I'd been given and to report on the way God had sustained me. But he was just as eager to report something to me. He told me that a few nights earlier some men from several local churches felt led to come together in our home for a time of prayer, and at the close they felt God leading them to form a British Full Gospel Businessmen's Fellowship. Minutes after officers were selected, the phone rang. An American voice said that he and another brother had just arrived at London airport and they wanted to help form a British FGBMFI! There was much laughing among the men, and then the Americans were told, "You're too late. We just did it ten minutes ago!"

In years to come, hundreds of chapters were formed throughout England, Ireland, Scotland, and Wales, and each year thousands of FGBMFI men and their families came together for a convention in Blackpool that resulted in many hearts and lives being renewed by the gospel of Jesus Christ.

I don't doubt for one moment that God used other praying men and women as well as ourselves to bring His plans into fruition. But how exciting to feel that one had a small part in a great work of God! Talk about "fullness of joy"! At His right hand there are indeed "pleasures forevermore" (Ps. 16:11)!

Tony was just one of many men whose lives were changed dramatically through this Holy Spirit movement. My shy, retiring husband became bolder to share the good news . . . and he even helped pass out Hungarian and Romanian Scripture portions during a holiday cruise up the Danube. He also gave a Bible and his testimony to a scientist during a Russian visit, even though his visa was canceled as a result and the authorities sent him packing a week early! My Tony, expelled from Russia for sharing the gospel! Now that's a miracle!

There was a terrible fire in an inner-city Manchester factory. The fire was in the upper floors of an old Victorian building and a number of women workers were trapped by iron bars over the windows, preventing their escape.

The picture in my mind, of those poor women, standing at the windows, looking out, screaming for help, haunted me night and day for weeks. My heart went out to them and I was tormented as if they were my own family.

Gradually I became aware of part of a verse that seemed to whisper to me,: "Fear not, for I have redeemed you; . . . You are Mine" (Isa. 43:1). After a day or two of "hearing" this loving promise, it occurred to me that God wanted to tell me something. This was not a new thing. For years it seemed that on occasions I would "hear" only part of a verse and that was my cue to then look up the fuller passage to learn what God wanted to say to me. Whether others heard the voice of God this way, I didn't know. I only know what happened to me.

Finally I picked up my Bible and searched the book of Isaiah, which I suspected held that passage. I found it in Isaiah chapter 43. The passage reads:

Thus says the LORD, who created you . . .
"Fear not; for I have redeemed you;
I have called you by your name;
You are Mine.

When you pass through the waters, I will be with you;
And through the rivers, they shall not overflow you.
When you walk through the fire, you shall not be
    burned,
Nor shall the flame scorch you." (vv. 1–2)

This was originally a word from God given to the prophet Isaiah to be passed on to the people of Israel. But I knew beyond a doubt that the same God who whispered those words to the prophet had spoken them into the hearts of many since then in troubled times—and now even to me. I wept to think of His love and care for such a person as myself. Not merely an ordinary sinner, but a profoundly unworthy one! Yet He called me by my name and said, "Fear not!"

I readily received His assurance that whatever flood or fire that came my way in the future I would have His protection. He was gently turning my grief for those women to a promise that I would not suffer that way. And I received comfort and assurance many times after that, from the glorious words given to the prophet, for God's mercy and care and compassion in every situation.

But the following summer something happened to remind me afresh of God's promise to me.

A few years earlier we had looked for a holiday home to which we could get away as a family before the boys got too old to want to travel with mum and dad. We found a wonderful little three-hundred-year-old cottage in Swaledale, Yorkshire Dales, and enjoyed visiting whenever possible. It was an idyllic spot, with scenery and stone architecture that looked like picture postcards brought to life.

One Sunday afternoon I was cooking in the tiny kitchen,

dropping doughnut batter into bubbling hot fat for the boys. My sleeve caught in the pan handle, and the next thing I knew the hot fat had covered my hand and sent streaks of pain up my arm. My hand quickly became swollen and my skin turned an unnatural color. All I could do was to pray, "Jesus . . . Jesus . . ."

A neighbor was a nurse and rushed over to look at the damage. She accompanied us as Tony drove across the moors into the next dale to find the doctor, but he was busy attending to a patient in a nearby farm, and so we had to wait for a long agonizing hour until he arrived. He bathed and medicated the hand, then carefully bandaged each badly burnt finger and finally the hand itself. He instructed us to return the following day so that he could examine it as he was concerned about infection.

Tony took our sons to church that evening to pray for me, leaving me alone in the cottage. I stood there and suddenly raised my painful, bandaged hand aloft and prayed, *I don't understand why this happened, Lord, but I praise You anyway!* Immediately the pain ceased—although it had been shooting up my arm constantly all afternoon and into the evening. All at once it felt as if the accident had never happened.

When Tony returned from church I told him, "You know, I think I have been healed!"

The following morning we once again took the car across the top of the moors and down into Wensleydale, to the surgery there. When the doctor removed the bandages, he looked at my *perfectly normal hand*, said there was no need for further bandages and dismissed me. Sadly, it was the other doctor in a group practice, so he did not know how badly burnt my hand actually was the afternoon before.

But our neighbor Mrs. Cherry knew, I thought, and on my return to the village I wanted to let her see for herself what God did for me. I knocked on her cottage door and showed her my unbandaged, unblemished hand. "See?" I said excitedly. "I've been healed!"

She looked at it and shrugged. "I guess it wasn't so bad after all," she said and turned away.

The following summer we were back in our small Yorkshire cottage, enjoying walking over the hills and discovering other villages nearby. One day I was walking on my own, high up in the mountain behind our cottage, and stopped to pick a field flower. I looked in wonder at the beautiful design of that tiny flower, which may have remained unnoticed if I had not picked it up. "Oh, Lord," I said aloud, "what a wonderful artist you are! You would even trouble to design this precious flower way up on this mountain!" And I couldn't help but stand there and worship Him.

A few days later I was in the village shop that was post office, grocery store, art supply store, and children's toy shop all in one. A sketchbook and pencils caught my eye, and I purchased them, almost without thinking. I hadn't done any sketching to speak of since my college days, when I drew caricatures for the university newspaper. I still don't know what I intended to do with them.

But later that day I found myself sitting on an old bench next to the stone-built village hall. The village looked like a dream in the sunshine, with a purple-hued backdrop of mountain and wooly sheep grazing on the slopes. I retrieved my new sketchbook and began to sketch the cottages that surrounded the humpback bridge and stream. I didn't yet know that that "accidental" trip to the village shop would begin another ministry, where sketches would be combined with written testimony to produce another avenue of witness that was freely available, even in a post-Christian culture like Britain.

CHAPTER SEVENTEEN

"Go home to your friends, and tell them what great things the Lord has done for you, and how He has had compassion on you" (Mark 5:19). I thought often about that verse that came to me after that golden summer in California. I had been learning, through the ministry of some of God's saints, that the Lord can more easily use someone who doesn't have his or her own agenda packed full of plans. He loves to use those who are "abiding in Him"—waiting and listening for His Spirit to divulge His plans. It would be wrong to interpret that as being fatalistic or even lazy. But my experiences in recent years were showing me that God wanted us to live in Him instead of rushing around madly and trying to organize His plans for Him. "God helps those who help themselves" seemed to me to be a nonsense that is sometimes said by people who have never learned to rest in Him.

When that Scripture first caught my attention, I didn't know just how I was to tell my friends. I didn't think of any particular way to spread the gospel, other than the weekly coffee mornings that continued to thrive at Copperfield. But within the next few months something strange seemed to be happening.

I began to wonder whether there was a way to spread the gospel in the British media. I was well aware of the restrictions on BBC and ITV against religious programming, and at the same time I noted that there were looser moral standards on TV than ever before. Already one brave woman, Mary Whitehouse, was getting constant abuse on TV and in the newspapers for her forthright stand against the lowering of moral standards, the increased sexual content in programs, the swearing and offensive language, even the curse words "Jesus Christ" all too familiarly creeping into the programs. Mary Whitehouse formed a National Viewers and Listeners Association and many Christians joined it, but apart from her name becoming a jest or a sneer used by comedians, there didn't seem any change in the quality of television programming.

I wondered whether the sort of interview format used so effectively in the USA could be adapted for use on British TV. Not of course with American hosts or guests, but with British men and women who would not be ashamed to be interviewed about their faith in Jesus Christ. One day I wrote to an American television evangelist and asked for prayer that somehow we might enjoy such an outreach in Britain.

To my amazement shortly afterward I received a letter from the PTL Network in Charlotte, North Carolina, from one of the vice presidents in charge of programming in other countries. PTL offered its programs to any countries willing to use them. Already there were PTL broadcasts in South American countries, Japan, some African states, and a few European spots. But not in Britain. The writer not only agreed to pray for us, he made us an amazing offer: choose an interviewer, gather together six or eight men and women as guests, and fly them to the USA where PTL would provide accommodation for all for a week and pay all the expenses of two pilot shows—including the design of a set specifically for use on British TV. I could hardly believe such generosity!

In a very short period of time, it seemed to me, God was

choosing His cast for what we decided to call the Good News broadcasts. Our close friend Roger Stanway, a Manchester lawyer, readily agreed to host the program and fly to the USA with us. The guests included a muscular farmer from Lancashire, a businessman from Bristol, a Catholic soloist. Three men and three women from a variety of denominations and walks of life were ready and eager to share their testimonies in Britain's first independent Christian television programs. I was asked to design a set which turned out to resemble an oak-beamed cottage with fireplace. Special music was written appropriate for the pilots.

All that was required of us, our generous friend explained, was to find our own airfares to Charlotte, North Carolina. The rest would be provided by PTL. When word got round to the various FGBMFI groups and churches in Britain, funds quickly came in, and in May 1982, an excited group of Brits (and one American) prepared to leave for the USA.

Hours before our flight, we were just seventy-five pounds short of our goal but we didn't doubt that this would be provided somehow. What we didn't expect were two letters that dropped through my mailbox that morning. One was a brochure from a travel company in Yorkshire I'd never heard of. Stamped on the large envelope was the name of the agency—Good News Travels! Coincidence? Surely not! The second letter was from a doctor friend who felt led to send us a check for seventy-five pounds! There was no doubt in anyone's mind that God was in this venture!

The week in Charlotte was a rare treat and an inspiring experience. But more than that, we all felt part of an exciting new witness that would touch many lives in Britain. When I first read that command of the Lord Jesus—"Go home to your friends"—little did I imagine that we might be used to pioneer such a project. As the week came to an end, we were presented with two large reels—two pilot programs that we hoped would be accepted for British television.

It was the beginning of a very disheartening chapter in our lives. The BBC turned us down flat, saying that according to their bylaws, such evangelical programs were forbidden. We thought of the first director general of the BBC, Scotsman John Reith, who arranged to have carved above the entrance to the BBC headquarters the slogan "To the Glory of God." What would he have thought of the direction of this company? We then sent the pilots to ITV Broadcasting, and then to the new Channel 4. Each repeated the mantra: no religious propaganda permitted! Never mind the propaganda that was being spewed out day and night of godless lifestyles, loose morals, and humanistic philosophies!

It was sometimes difficult to understand God's ways. "My thoughts are not your thoughts, nor are your ways My ways" was a text that was hard to accept those days (Isa. 55:8). Many letters were written to newspapers (at least Britain still enjoyed freedom of the press) and as some of us traveled round the country, trying to share our vision, many Christians admitted the need for more godly programming. I recall in some meetings asking the audience, "How many of you would want Christian programs on TV? Raise your hands." They all held up their hands. Then, "How many of you write letters to the BBC or ITV requesting this?" No hands went up. I then asked, "How many of you have been offended by programs you have watched?" Many raised their hands. Finally, "How many of you have written letters of complaint about this?" And only one or two hands went up.

I thought of the popular American series *Dallas* that had evoked a storm of protest when the British broadcasters decided to change the timing of the weekly show. Thousands of Brits wrote in or phoned their complaints. The result: the broadcasters changed their minds and gave in to the protests! Yet when many British Christians were denied all but a half-hour weekly hymn-singing program, they remained quiet. And when scores of unsuitable program themes and dialogue were shown every week, few bothered to protest. I felt this British reserve and tolerance could sometimes be an enemy of Christian witness.

In time the pilots were used on the new cable stations that had begun to spring up. But to this day no independent evangelical programs are permitted on the major British networks. Even when a Christian theme is presented in a documentary, broadcasters are careful to present a "balanced" picture, with those who are opposed to the message providing their strong anti-Christian views. However, when there's a documentary of the work of atheistic scientist Richard Dawkins, or of Steven Hawking, there's no such "balance" produced with Christian scholars allowed to present another point of view.

God surely had His reasons for uniting us in this television venture, even though it did not produce the results we hoped for. But it caused me to consider another avenue which was open to us and which we did not use at all.

CHAPTER EIGHTEEN

The next year as the FGBMFI convention in Blackpool approached, there were discussions about how to advertise the event more effectively. I suggested buying a full page of a British newspaper and filling it with testimonies of men and woman who found Christ through the FGBMFI. I had been involved in newspaper layouts in college and in my publishing career in the USA. I thought it would be effective to design the page to look like every other newspaper page, with articles and pictures presented in the newspaper's own format. We found that we could purchase a page for £2,500. Not a single protest was made by the news staff that "religious propaganda was forbidden."

It was our first experience with the printed media and further pages were purchased when Billy Graham came to Manchester the following year. We sought funds from local churches and quickly received sufficient to buy three pages in newspapers, publicizing the Crusade but more important, publicizing the conversion experiences of local men and women who came to Christ through similar meetings.

Throughout that difficult period of struggle with British broadcasting, I learned a valuable lesson about using one's talents where one can. If one door closes, try another. Television remained off-limits to Christian programming, but we soon learned that evangelizing through newspapers was an untapped resource. And it also developed into writing testimonies for church bulletins, or Christian newspapers and journals.

One day as I was reading Hebrews 11, that wonderful faith chapter, I thought again of the diversity of backgrounds of the saints listed there. "Strangers and pilgrims" (v. 13) was the description of these men and women who were willing to give their lives for the love of God. It occurred to me that a book of modern saints would be a great witness to folk today who didn't read the Bible. I knew similar books had been written in times past; some of these were on my parents' shelves and I read bits of them when I was a child. Now that would be a worthwhile project, I thought, for someone to do today!

The following year I was asked to ghost write the testimony of an Australian woman, formerly a television host, who had found faith in Christ and was now a dynamic evangelist. I had begun writing interviews and short stories for Christian journals and newspapers in the UK but this was my first venture into book writing. In years to come I wrote the story of judo champion Owen Lowery, who fell and broke his neck in a charity match and was led to Christ by judo sportsmen who visited him in the hospital. Later, stories came to my attention from a part of the globe I never imagined I would visit someday . . .

CHAPTER NINETEEN

Over the years, as my long-lost daughter became a teenager, I thought of her. Then as she entered her twenties, I thought of her. Of course I silently celebrated every one of her birthdays when the second of July came around. Then sometime in the 1970s and into the '80s, I allowed myself a little fantasy once in a while. I'd imagine that the phone would ring, and I would pick it up. On the other end was an unfamiliar voice, and it said "Mrs. Holland? This is Susan Joseph . . ." Sometimes I'd dwell on this make-believe encounter and think how glorious it would feel. Other times I'd snap back to reality and give myself a talking to. How foolish!

But in our home, we never discussed that incident of 1955, when I gave away my first child. Of course Tony hadn't forgotten, and I certainly had not, but we never discussed it. In fact it was rather bizarre: if we were sitting together in an evening, watching a drama on television, and a mother was going through the trauma of surrendering her child, we would not comment. We'd look straight ahead at the screen and pretend there was nothing special about the topic. I never had the courage to turn to Tony, look him in the eyes, and say "Doesn't that remind you of my experience?" I could *not* discuss it! There was not a single other subject that we refrained from sharing with each other. But only that one was "out of bounds."

As my own daughter was approaching her twenty-ninth birthday in 1984, another adopted daughter named Susan was entering her twenties. My sister's beautiful blonde daughter—whom Irene had inexplicably also named Susan—was about to marry a Christian college student named Brad. Although we had seen little of Irene's family in recent years, she wrote to us about the forthcoming wedding and said Susan wanted to invite her cousins Jon and Chris as groomsmen. Chris had started a new job and thought it would be difficult to get off during that time, but Jon was eager to attend. So was I, and I wrote to Irene that both Jon and I would love to fly over for the occasion. Oddly enough, Irene replied that they would only be able to have Jon. It was another one of those mysterious gestures. But I was glad that sixteen-year-old Jonathan was able to take his first solo trip to the USA and be with the family once again.

Early in 1984, I planned a return to the USA that would be an exceptional occasion—I was taking my sister-in-law, Margaret, on her first trip to America that October. A retired headmistress, she was very excited to be taking this long-awaited trip. I would be her personal tour guide around the eastern states. We'd take the Greyhound bus just as I had done a decade earlier with my sons during our California summer. I planned to visit friends and family, and particularly visit Irene and Don who now had a pastorate in Ohio. We'd wind up in Allentown, the place of my birth, to visit more family members. Sadly my dear mother had died several years earlier and this would be my first trip to the USA without staying with her.

Having had some unfortunate experiences with Irene in years past, I decided to deflect similar problems by approaching her first about our schedule. I let her know I was planning a three-week trip to the eastern states, stopping to visit cousins and friends from Virginia to New York. I wrote that I knew she and Don had busy schedules, so that I wanted her to tell me when during those three weeks she could have us visit her and how long she might want us. I said we would work around her schedule, to make sure it suited their plans. After hearing from her, I could then write to other friends and family and arrange our twenty-one-day bus tour.

Around that same time I was thinking about Sue Joseph again, and a thought occurred to me. It had now been twenty-nine years since her birth, and one day on the spur of the moment I decided to write to Irene's friend Jean Brobst whose back garden adjoined the Joseph's. Why not tell her about Sue? I could ask if she could tell me any news. And so I wrote a brief letter and eagerly awaited a reply. When Jean wrote back, she remarked that somehow she wasn't surprised that I was Susan's mother. She told me that the Josephs had left Emmaus some years earlier. But she knew that Sue had married someone in the local Lutheran Church and was now living and studying in New Orleans.

I was excited to hear that news and days later decided to do something about it. I wrote a brief note to "The Pastor, Lutheran Church, Emmaus, Pennsylvania, USA." I told him that Sue's birth was the best thing that could have happened to me, as it brought me home to Christ. I said I would love to know more about her, if he were willing.

But months passed, and I never heard from him. "Okay, Lord," I said to Him. "I guess You don't want me to go any further with this."

One day that summer I received a phone call from May, a church friend. She asked me if I would speak at a ladies' dinner meeting she was organizing, and the date was July 2. When I heard the date, the day of Sue's birthday, I sensed immediately that it was time to speak publicly about Sue's birth and how it changed my life. I felt convinced that this was God's time, but I was anxious about Tony's reaction. I didn't have the courage to tell him my plans, because I suspected he'd try to talk me out of it.

It was not easy speaking about this very personal event even to a group of women, many of whom I knew. Of course it would have been impossible to discuss it in 1955, when one simply did not share such things. But now, in 1984, there was more talk of pregnancies outside of marriage, and regrettably, it was now almost such a common occurrence that younger people wondered what all the fuss was about. The dynamic change in moral codes in a few short decades seemed inconceivable to those of my age.

But God gave me the courage to speak freely about how such a devastating experience could be turned to good when I reached out to God and became a new creature in Christ. After the meeting, I was surprised when several women came up to me to report similar experiences. One confessed that the birth had been a scar that never healed; another said she was unable to move on from the traumatic experience. They said this night's talk had encouraged them to seek God's healing and learn from it.

One woman said to me, "Will you meet Sue someday?"

I laughed. "Probably not here on earth, but I hope in heaven!"

She insisted, "Oh, you must meet her, you must!"

A few days later I received a phone call from another woman who had attended the dinner, and she told me she had a dream that I was going to meet Sue. I was touched by her message.

On Friday of that week, I suddenly felt the urge to attend the FGBMFI Saturday breakfast meeting at the Manchester Airport hotel where they were held. We hadn't attended regularly for a few years, as other Christian commitments began to alter our schedules. Tony had been national treasurer in the early years, but had eventually passed the job on to others. Now, suddenly, I felt we ought to go. Tony agreed.

The following morning we crowded into the familiar hotel dining room with people from a variety of denominations who met for fellowship and an inspiring talk. The speaker used a strange text from the gospel of Luke, about Zacharias, and how he had been struck dumb until his son John was born. I cannot recall much of the message that morning, but I began to weep. I was so moved I could not stop shaking. I kept looking at that text in my Bible, and then across the page to the portion about Mary being told about her forthcoming delivery, and how she silently "pondered [all those things] in her heart" (Luke 2:19). I underscored both passages and wrote in the margin "keeping silence until the time came." And I could not stop weeping.

"What was that all about?" Tony asked me on the way home.

"I don't know, it just moved me so much. I just felt blessed and shaken at the same time . . ."

Sunday morning, July 8, 1984. It was usually a rush to prepare ourselves for church, with the boys invariably dragging their feet and being the last ones in the car. But this Sunday we arrived early, and it gave me time to sit and meditate for a few moments. I took up my Bible, and it fell open to Isaiah 54. I began to read at verse four.

> Fear not; for thou shalt not be ashamed: neither be
> thou confounded; for thou shalt not be put to shame: for
> thou shalt forget the shame of thy youth, and shalt not

remember the reproach of thy widowhood any more. . . .

For the LORD hath called thee as a woman forsaken and grieved in spirit, and a wife of youth, when thou wast refused, saith thy God.

For a small moment have I forsaken thee; but with great mercies will I gather thee.

In a little wrath I hid my face from thee for a moment; but with everlasting kindness will I have mercy on thee, saith the LORD thy Redeemer. (Isa. 54:4, 6–8 KJV)

It was one of those moments of special clarity when one knows something powerful has happened—one senses that God Himself has spoken personally. I looked around me. Who was that for, I wondered. I looked across the aisle to a friend whose husband had just left her, and I thought perhaps the passage was a word from the Lord to comfort her. I rushed over and put a note in her hand. "This is for you!"

But even as I returned to my seat, and the service started, I wondered. Was it perhaps for someone else? Was I being precipitous again, as Tony often described me?

That afternoon after our meal together, the boys clamored upstairs to their rooms, and Tony retired to the garden, to sit and doze under the laburnum tree. I had just finished putting everything in the dishwasher when the telephone rang.

"Mrs. Holland?" said a sweet unfamiliar voice. "This is Susan Joseph."

Vicki and Sue's reunion, 1984

SUE

Sue in England with John and kids, 1997

Reunion with Vicki, Irene (middle), and Sue, 2004

CHAPTER TWENTY

"Oh no, no, it couldn't be . . ." I gasped.

"I got the letter you sent to our former pastor in Emmaus," she began.

"No! No! I can't believe it! Is it really you?"

And by this time we were both weeping with joy. "I have wanted to find you for years," Sue said. "My mother . . . er, Betty . . . had always said she'd help me find you. Then some years ago we read something in the Allentown newspaper about you moving to England. We knew your husband was a university professor, but we couldn't recall where. We used to say we should fly to London and walk the streets, searching for a woman who looked like me."

By this time we were weeping and laughing at the same time. "I didn't think the pastor wanted us to pursue anything," I explained. "I thought perhaps he might not have approved."

"Oh, not at all; he passed the letter to my parents, but it somehow got lost on my dad's desk for months," she said.

I had thought all those years that my name would be banned within the Joseph family. I no doubt got that impression because my sister would not discuss the fact that her two children were born to other women. I recall a time when someone innocently asked her about their "real" parents. Irene was furious. "They are *our* children! *We* are their real parents!" Don added hotly, "They are our flesh and blood!" Perhaps I imagined that all adopted parents would be similarly sensitive and unwilling to acknowledge the birth parents. I didn't dream that Betty Joseph was actually happy to help Sue find me.

And so we spoke, wept, laughed, and shared many things in that first amazing conversation. I told her we were planning to visit the USA in October. She said she couldn't wait that long and would love to visit me before then. My head was spinning—whatever would Tony say?

We must have spoken for an hour, and I was thinking about her phone bill, but then Jonathan came down the stairs and looked at me curiously. He noted I had been simultaneously laughing and crying. "What's wrong, mum?" he asked.

"Jonathan, it's your sister, Sue!" and I handed him the phone. He looked shocked, then pleased, and grabbed the phone. I had told both sons a year or two earlier about their secret sister. I could not bring myself to admit to Tony that I had shared that information with them.

"Hi, Sue!" Jon said, and then began to answer questions put to him by his brand-new, twenty-nine-year-old sister. She must have said something about his accent because he next laughed and said indignantly, "Like the Beatles? Certainly not! They are Liverpudlians, while I"—he added proudly—"am from Manchester!" Sue couldn't have known of the age-old rivalry between the young men of those northern cities spaced scarcely thirty miles apart.

But we had not yet finished making our important arrangements to get together, and I was impatient to grab the phone back from him. As we spoke of our plans, Sue said it would suit her to come to England in August, for two weeks, to finally meet her family . . . but especially the mother who thought she would never see her again. I was sorry to hear that Sue had been divorced for some years, but secretly glad that I would be able to entertain her all on her own.

My head kept spinning as I hung up the receiver and turned away from that extraordinary conversation. I thought of the heart's cry of the prodigal's father: my child was lost and is found (Luke 15:32). I could scarcely believe what had happened; but I had to believe it. She had contacted me! God had brought her back to me!

I recalled the strange events of the day before, when I could not stop weeping as I looked at those verses about Zacharias, struck dumb until the child was delivered, and Mary, keeping all those wonders silently in her heart. Why had those two passages caused such a storm in my soul?

And then that Scripture in Isaiah, of the rejected young woman:

> Thou shalt forget the shame of thy youth, and shalt not remember the reproach of thy widowhood any more . . . For the LORD hath called thee as a woman forsaken and grieved in spirit, and a wife of youth, when thou wast refused . . . For a small moment have I forsaken thee; but with great mercies will I gather thee. (Isa. 54:4, 6–7 KJV)

These verses were crowding themselves into my already dazed mind as I made my way out the door and into the garden where Tony was dozing comfortably beneath the laburnum tree. There was a moment of panic, when I thought I could not bring myself to approach him with the news.

"Guess who was just on the phone?" I asked him as he stirred. He looked at me blankly.

"Susan Joseph." And as the long-hidden words escaped my lips I began to feel a new strength.

"What does she want?" he looked at me and frowned.

"She wants to meet me, of course!"

"But I thought it was all dead and buried . . ." he said coldly.

"Well, *she* isn't dead and buried!"

"Why now? It just doesn't seem . . ."

"Do you think I should wait another twenty-nine years to see her? Should she have to wait another twenty-nine years to see me?" By now, I was ready to go to war to bring Sue into our lives.

But Tony was talking of embarrassment, humiliation, and what would his sister think.

"Well, she will have to know all about it, after all these years, because she and I will be visiting Sue in Allentown in October!"

"Oh no." Tony sat up, ready for battle. "She must not be told! I just won't have it!"

"Tony, we have arranged to meet in October when I take your sister to the States. It would be absurd to go there and be prevented from sharing with Margaret this incredible news. How could I do that? That's too much to ask of me."

I recalled his wonderful reaction to my confession, twenty-seven years earlier. He must have been devastated to learn about my child, but after a brief moment, he had said, "If Jesus forgave you, I can do no less." How was it possible that he was so forgiving and generous then, and now so humiliated?

We spent some time wrestling with the matter, Tony agitated and even suspicious of her motives, while I was equally determined and impatient to embrace my child and accept any accompanying embarrassment. Finally I felt we'd argued the point long enough, and I returned to the house to plan for her forthcoming visit. I had enough trouble trying to convince Tony about my visit to her in October; I thought I'd better wait a few days until broaching the subject of her visit to Copperfield that next month.

The next day I drove into Manchester, still in shock, feeling positively unsafe behind the wheel, as I was still numb with joy, still unbalanced from the news. I floated around Kendall Milne's Department Store in a daze, finally ending in the greeting card department. The tears flowed as I searched for an appropriate card. What would the clerk say if I asked her, "Excuse me, but do you have a birthday card for a daughter you haven't seen in twenty-nine years?" I finally settled for a more generic one.

I was comforted by both Chris's and Jon's reactions to the news of a sister coming into the family. They were anxious to learn more about her and were fascinated when a few days later photographs, a cassette tape, and long letters arrived in a bundle. We sat around the cassette recorder and played the tape, all three of us in awe, hearing her sweet voice. I had not yet resumed discussions with Tony. In the coming days it seemed he was brooding about a great disappointment, as if I had been unfaithful to him. It was a barrier that we'd never before experienced in twenty-seven years of marriage.

Although I was upset and disappointed at his reaction, another part of me was determined to dwell on the joyous discovery of my long-lost daughter and the exquisite reunions soon to take place. There was still the delicate matter of his sister, Margaret, having to be told. I had not backed down on that—it would be impossible for me to meet Sue in October without Margaret's knowledge.

Toward the end of that week I had the strangest dream of my life . . . *I was in our bedroom looking down on a trunk I found beside my bed. I sensed I needed to open it, but I needed help. At that moment I heard Tony slowly walking up the stairs at the other end of the hallway. Good, I thought, he'll come and help move this. But as he reached the top of the stairs, instead of turning right to approach our bedroom, he turned left and walked into the boys' bathroom. At the same time, he put his hand over his eyes as if to shield them. I waited some moments for him to come out and then hoped he would walk toward our room. But when he left the bathroom he again shielded his eyes with his hand, turned, and walked back down the stairs. Disappointed, I knew I would have to open the trunk myself. But when I did, I discovered it was a coffin, and a small body was lying in it! Stunned, I looked down helplessly and didn't know what to do! At that moment, the body moved and came to life!*

That next moment Tony and I were in our car in the lane next to our house. I was driving and that little girl from the trunk was standing in the lane in front of us. I knew what I had to do, and so I aimed the car to run over her . . .

I was horrified when I awoke. The meaning was abundantly clear. But contrary to the dream, I was more determined than ever to welcome my daughter wholeheartedly, whatever the cost.

That night I told Tony of my dream. He was shocked and merely went back to his reading, puffing on his pipe. But before we went to bed, he said, "When are you going to tell Margaret?" I knew I had won!

Sundays we regularly drove the boys down to South Cheshire after church for Sunday lunch with Margaret and her husband, Joe. This time I was prepared to clear the air. After lunch I drew Margaret aside and said, "I'm afraid I have some shocking news for you . . ."

"Aren't we going to the States? Has something happened?"

"Oh no, not that. We're going all right. But I have something to tell you that I have kept a secret for many years . . ." and I proceeded to give her a summary of what happened in 1955 up until that wonderful phone call of the previous week.

"Is that all?" Margaret laughed. "You forget I've been a teacher all my life and I've seen everything. There's nothing that anyone does that surprises me! I think it's wonderful, and I shall love meeting her!'

During subsequent phone calls and letters, my daughter and I learned even more about each other. I had begun my BA studying drama and completed it in English. So had Sue. We both did our Master's degrees in English. She and I both have a great love of the English classical writers, classical music (Rachmaninoff is our favorite composer), and we both enjoy sketching and painting. We both love singing. I would marvel each time a letter arrived in the postbox with the now familiar signature on the envelope. I marveled because her handwriting was so similar to my own!

I had eagerly written to Irene that first week to tell her the extraordinary news of Sue's phone call and our forthcoming reunions. I described our many similarities, how pleased the boys were with their new sister, and the preparations that I was making to welcome her to Copperfield. Above all, I wrote, I am so thrilled that she calls me "Mom!"

So when Irene's letter dropped through the mailbox the following week, I couldn't wait to read it. But with growing shock and dismay I read her diatribe about me seeking to take her away from her adopted parents! *You have no right for her to call you "Mom!"* she wrote. *A mother is not just someone that gives birth. She spends a lifetime looking after the child and sacrificing all for it. It's a disgrace for her to call you that!* And the rest of the letter was in the same vein. It was so cruel that I didn't want it in my hands a moment longer, and I quickly ripped it up and discarded it.

My heart was pumping wildly. It was such a hurtful letter, I found it difficult to breathe. My friends in England rejoiced with me to learn of Sue's appearance. Why would my own sister try to spoil my joy at such a time? I could not believe that her own failure to conceive had twisted her thinking to such an extent. After all, she could not have borne two more lovely children than Susan and Donald. They were such a credit to her!

But a letter that arrived a few days later raised my spirits more than I could imagine. It was from Betty Joseph. I anxiously wondered what she would say to me. For years I assumed that she would not take kindly to me invading her family circle.

When I opened it, it began: *Dear Sister in Love,*

We have thanked God for you every day since you gave us Susan...

It was difficult to keep the tears from flowing as I read her loving letter of gratitude and joy at knowing Sue and I would now meet. She told me of her own efforts to help Sue find me. When Sue was fourteen, Betty had told her as much as she knew about me and said that, when the time was right and Sue wanted to pursue it, she would do all she could to help her find me. What a woman! I will never forget her.

I began to prepare the guest room for the arrival of my beloved daughter. An old divan was in place that opened into a double bed when guests came, but I wanted to make the room more personal, more feminine for her. I removed the divan and brought in a twin bed. I covered it with orchid-colored blankets and then topped it with a lace tablecloth. Some lace pillows and a doll completed the scene. I'd sit in the room for hours, contemplating her visit, thinking of the many talks we'd have. In just four weeks, she'd be with me!

A week or so later a postcard arrived from Sue, with just a quick note on it. At first I didn't understand it. It read: *Just met a wonderful guy named Dennis, and we got married! With his work making it impossible to come in August as planned, we'll have to make it next summer. But of course we'll meet in October. Be happy for me! Love, Sue.*

I was devastated. Not to see her! Not to have her to myself! I was so distressed I hid the card from Tony and the boys. I couldn't bring myself to admit the news for days. I feared they'd think she was impulsive, untrustworthy. More than that, I felt I didn't matter as much anymore. She hadn't signed the card "lots of love" as before. Just "love." No doubt her "lots of love" was now reserved for Dennis what's his name. I was heartbroken! Had I meant so little to her after all?

After Tony drove off to work and the boys went to school, I'd go into "Sue's room" and mourn her loss. Of course she would still visit me and I would visit her, but I would have to share her. And although I wouldn't want her to remain single, I so longed to have her to myself for just a little while!

On the second or third day later, as I was moping around, so discouraged, I recalled that incident in the lawyer's office back in July 1955, when I had to sign the preliminary papers for Sue's adoption. I was sitting in the chair opposite the lawyer, when the nurse behind me suddenly reached down and put the baby into my arms! A sob escaped me, and at the same time the lawyer motioned for me to sign the papers. So I lifted her up and gave her back to the nurse. I couldn't understand why that happened.

Almost twenty years later I was reading a powerful book about inner healing written by the sister of ex-President Jimmy Carter, Ruth Carter Stapleton. She wrote examples of people who were hurt or grieving and how God healed them through visualizing Jesus into their traumatic situations. As she wrote of one young person damaged by an incident that happened many years earlier, I began to weep. And at that moment, as in a vision, I saw myself back in the lawyer's office, holding up my baby, to return her to the nurse's arms. But when I looked up, it was not the nurse standing there—it was Jesus! And I gave her into His arms.

I wept for all those years I had not known my daughter, but I wept most of all for the knowledge that she had been in His arms all along. What a relief, a joy, to know this!

I turned back to the book and resumed reading. Mrs. Stapleton continued: *Visualize Jesus into the situation that has been troubling you . . .*

I cried aloud: "I just did!"

It was a healing so unexpected, that I marvel about it still. When God touches you without you even asking Him, you know it is His work alone. From that day onward, I was more convinced than ever before, that God was fulfilling His promise to me—to bless her—when I had prayed for her as she lay in my arms that first day in the hospital.

Now as I sat in my guest room, full of self-pity and selfish longing, I remembered why I was so miserable. I wanted to take her back! But she no longer belonged to me. And now I had to hand her over to Jesus once again, if I wanted my peace restored.

Not long after reading Ruth Stapleton's book, I confided in a doctor friend. When I admitted being perplexed about the nurse giving me the baby, she smiled. "That's a common procedure so that there are witnesses that you are willingly relinquishing your rights." Ah, so it was a sign of surrender!

And now, once more, foolish slow-to-learn Vicki had to grasp that lesson all over again. Would I ever get it? I recalled that cryptic comment of the Lord Jesus to his slow-to-learn disciples: "He who clings to his life (or child or possessions?) will lose it, but he who willingly relinquishes it will keep it for eternity."

I finally realized that the only way I would have the right relationship with Sue in the future was to recognize that she first of all belonged to the Lord Jesus, then to her partner, and finally to me.

It is a lesson every parent is obliged to learn, often painfully, when their son or daughter falls in love and wishes to marry. Even those Christian parents who went through a baptismal or dedication ceremony when their child was born have to repeat that pledge of commitment and renunciation, over and over, when their child grows to adulthood and chooses a career or a spouse, or moves to another country.

I was learning that a parent will always lose out by holding on and that a child flourishes best when the parent respects the choices his child makes. It was a lesson I had to learn with Sue now, and again and again with sons Chris and Jon, as they moved into adulthood. But it is always such a painful one!

The clouds parted and the sun shone again in the days that followed. I told Tony and the boys that Sue was now married. Of course it never affected them as it did me. And in the days to come I disassembled "Sue's room" and made it once again a generic guest room. As it remained when Sue—and Dennis—shared it the following year.

CHAPTER TWENTY-TWO

The anticipation of our trip to the USA grew as I considered the glorious climax of the visit—meeting my long-lost daughter after an absence of twenty-nine years. The excitement was somewhat marred by the thought of Irene's angry reply to my letter. How would she receive me now? Would she ask about Sue or would she ignore the topic completely, pretending that she didn't exist? How would she treat Margaret, who was only an innocent bystander in this sisterly combat? What saddened me most of all was the possibility that Margaret would witness a hostile atmosphere, when I'd prayed that she would see only Christian love and acceptance.

As the summer wore on, many letters and phone calls traveled between Sue and me. I could scarcely think of anything else! I would finally see her!

It was only as the bus took us closer to Irene's home in Cedarville, Ohio, that I became sick with worry. What would she say? I often recalled over the years my mother's disapproval (justified in most cases) of my behavior, my thoughtlessness of others, my only concern being my comfort and enjoyment. But after a precious month in 1980 spent nursing her during her final battle with cancer, we shared so much love and understanding that it wiped out all the tension and acrimony either of us had all those years. I treasured her final weeks as we sat and talked quietly together, and she sometimes sang an old gospel song that stuck in her mind:

I'm longing to go, I'm longing to go,
There's nothing no nothing to keep me below,
When the trumpet shall sound to my mansion on high,
I'll leave without saying good-bye . . .

Now it seemed that that old disapproval I often felt from my mother had taken up residence in her elder daughter. Almost three decades after Sue's birth, it seemed Irene was doing her best to make me keep paying for it. I leaned toward Margaret as we were approaching our final stop: "How much do you want to bet Irene will change her mind about how long we can stay?"

At the same time, I had to admit that God allows certain difficulties into our lives for a reason. I thought of Joseph, when he saw his brothers after many years. "You meant evil against me," he told them, "but God meant it for good" (Gen. 50:20). Irene hadn't sold me into slavery, but she had a way of making her disapproval strongly felt without saying a word! And once again I knew it was up to me to trust God in whatever awaited me in Cedarville.

As we alighted from the bus, before we set our luggage on the floor, Irene greeted us with, "Before we go home, you'll have to go to the counter and have your tickets changed. You'll have to leave Saturday as we have something else on for Sunday."

This change of plans meant we'd have to leave Saturday night and spend the night on the bus, which was not what we'd wanted. I had hoped to cross the Blue Ridge Mountains of Virginia in the daytime, giving us the best view of that beautiful area. Instead we'd travel in those mountains in pitch dark. It was just one more sample of Irene's perverse need to control what others planned.

Those three days in her home that year were so painful that I have mercifully forgotten many details. She was cold and aloof, speaking with me as little as possible. She did not mention my daughter. At one point I struggled to breathe, as I said, "Irene, you make me feel so unwelcome!"

She looked at me and said, "That's your problem."

At that moment Margaret came into the room and said she felt we should leave. How thankful I was for my sister-in-law! We left the house and spent the next few hours in that small town trying to deflect the stress and disappointment I felt. I dreaded returning to the house—and remaining until the Saturday. Under the circumstances I began to be thankful that the visit was cut short.

That Saturday Irene asked Susan and Brad, who lived nearby, to drive us to the bus station. It was a quick dismissal that left me stunned. I loved Susan and Brad, a sweet couple, but I sensed that this was a delicate situation. I assumed Irene gave them her own version of my prodigal past and plans to meet my daughter. I learned much later that she had told them not a word about our long-awaited reunion. (Perhaps she feared giving Susan ideas of her own.) But Irene had not failed to tell her daughter about my past life and the disgrace I brought on my family. Thus our brief time with the young couple was an awkward one. I regretted this so much.

The day we left Irene's home I recalled the verse where Jesus said, "If the household is worthy, let your peace come upon it . . . And whoever will not receive you nor hear your words, when you depart from that house or city, shake off the dust from your feet" (Matt. 10:13-14). As I crossed the threshold on my way out, I wondered whether I would ever see them again. It began an estrangement that lasted seventeen years.

What was so unpardonable about Irene's behavior was what it did to Margaret. My sister-in-law was an occasional churchgoer but did not share Tony's and my strong commitment to Jesus. I had hoped and prayed this visit to my many Christian friends would be a witness of our faith. But Margaret's first words after we boarded the bus and settled into our seats was, "Well! If *that's* being a Christian . . . !" Yes, Irene was a Baptist minister's wife and Don, a preacher of the gospel. But there was something going on in their lives that was baffling. How could she be so deliberately inhospitable? How could Don go along with this? I couldn't understand it and admitted the same to Margaret. However, I reminded her of all the other incredibly generous Christian friends who had opened their hearts and homes to us. I only hoped she would take those happy memories home with her.

But now I had to put that gloomy experience behind me. I was drained emotionally with Irene's rejection but I resolved to not let it mar the wonderful reunion to come. Just then a delightful thing happened. I looked out the window of the bus the very moment a car was passing us, and the license plate bore this slogan:

You've Got a Friend in Pennsylvania

Oh yes, Lord, I cried silently, I have many friends in Pennsylvania! My dear cousins Mimi and Grace, and then finally my darling daughter who I will hold in my arms within a few days! The slogan was a playful little message from God assuring me of countless blessings He had bestowed on me all my life and, to top it all, that the lost daughter would become my dearest friend for the rest of my life!

We made stops in Virginia to visit lifelong friends, then to Washington, DC, so that Margaret could tour the Capital, and finally to Philadelphia, to visit my Weiss and Harley relatives living in that area.

Early on the morning of October 24, 1984, my cousin Grace drove Margaret and me to the Joseph home in the west end of Allentown. We drove past lush wooded areas and sprawling houses surrounded by gardens, a world away from the row houses on narrow streets in which I had been raised. Then we pulled over in front of a handsome modern home. It was like a dream—I got out of the car and saw in a blur this tiny young woman running down the driveway to meet me. And then she was in my arms, with the sweet scent of her hair at my face. I held her thinking it was the best day of my life—more wondrous than my wedding day or the birth of my sons. The lost was found!

And again I recalled the passage I had read the morning of her phone call: "I hid my face from thee for a moment; but with everlasting kindness will I have mercy on thee" (Isa. 54:8). Dennis took our photograph there in the driveway, as we looked in each other's faces for the first time.

After introducing Sue to cousin Grace and Margaret, we arranged to meet up later in the day, and they left. Sue and I went into the house where Betty Joseph was waiting. It was another moving experience to meet up with the woman who had become mother to my daughter and was now my "sister-in-love." She and I immediately forged a friendship and bond that few women experience.

Sue looked so much younger than I imagined. She had a lovely face, a long mane of curly brown hair, a tiny figure. She was not quite five feet tall. She had a wonderful, bright personality and wanted to show me all her photo albums from her earliest years, explaining in detail each relative on Abe's side of the family, then Betty's. Although I loved to look at her baby pictures and those of her as a young child and then a teenager, I longed desperately to have her all to myself. I was very pleased to have met Betty, but what I wanted most in the world was to be alone with Sue and to begin to know all about her. I had satisfactorily dispensed with Grace and Margaret for the day; but here were Betty and Dennis, and I wondered how I might tactfully suggest that Sue and I drive somewhere on our own.

Somehow I struggled through that first day, surrounded by Sue's new husband and her other mother. We even drove to visit Betty's family some miles away, where I tried my best to be enthusiastic in greeting them all. Part of me felt very unsure of my position in the group. It was as if I'd lost my identity somewhere.

The following day, at long last, Sue and I managed to drive off on our own. I was able to share with her some of my childhood, as we drove past the humble little house on Cedar Street where I lived as a young child and then the row house on Liberty Street where I lived in those troubled teen years.

There were a host of similarities that amazed us. It was a delight to learn how alike we were in many ways. Our love of literature, of classical music, and of art was a remarkable discovery. Tony and I had always hoped our sons would learn to appreciate good music or maybe even become musicians. We had hoped they would go to university and get degrees. We had sent them to the best private schools to give them opportunities to succeed academically. But they went their own way, choosing other careers. The irony was that the one child I did not raise was the one who seemed to follow my choices more closely. It's a funny old world.

CHAPTER TWENTY-THREE

I would have been happier spending two or three days with Sue in a hotel somewhere, but our tight schedule meant that after a brief day and night together we would say our farewells the following day until her promised visit the following summer. I painfully said good-bye to my sweet, pretty daughter, feeling perhaps I needed her love more than she needed mine. After all, she had a new husband and parents who adored their only child. She had a network of adopted families, like Betty and Abe, and a life of studying in New Orleans which made her very happy.

She assured me that she (and Dennis) would come to England for a few weeks the next summer, and she invited me to visit her in New Orleans as soon as possible. Meanwhile we agreed to write and phone and tape messages in an effort to fill in the gaps of our twenty-nine year separation.

Returning to England after such a memorable reunion, I was happy to relate my experiences to the boys and Tony. My dear husband indignantly took to heart Irene's inhospitable treatment of me. He was always my chief supporter and defender, particularly when it came to Irene. I was glad to be home again: England had always been a comfort and welcome whenever I returned from the States. And quickly settling into my usual routines at church and in the home, I learned to enjoy my new relationship with Sue without the heartache of possessiveness. We would meet again soon. Her letters quickly resumed and we were feeling comfortable with each other as our love grew.

There was one area in which we could not agree. Sometimes in our letters there came an element of debate as Sue told me of her passion for astrology. I felt the subject was not only invalid but that it was unchristian. I felt that her pursuit of it could jeopardize her developing Christian faith. She had a genuine love of God and of His earthly manifestation, Jesus. She had a touching capacity for forgiveness and acceptance of those who may have wronged her. She was a modern young woman, not naive or foolish, but there was a sweet simplicity about her that I loved. But this preoccupation with astrology worried me, and I wondered how I could draw her away from this unsuitable subject. I felt it was an obsession that could be harmful.

I realized one thing about Sue as we continued our correspondence: she was not one to give up on any convictions she held dear. She tried all the harder to convince me of the value of the subject. And as hard as I tried to dissuade her, that's how hard she fought to show me I was wrong. It soon became a small worry to see her letters drop through the postbox. I wondered what new argument she would give me and how I would counter that. I began to pray about how to answer the letters and how I could do so without hurting our relationship.

I had always felt that I was more like my mother than my father. My father—and indeed the entire Weiss family—were gentle people who never criticized others, never argued or raised their voices. A Weiss reunion was about the quietest event imaginable! Harley reunions, on the other hand, were full of laughter and shouting and arguing. My mother was a colorful character who spoke her mind and didn't hesitate to correct a person she felt was wrong. As a child I recall many times when she scolded

Irene or me while Daddy kept quiet. "Am I right, Allen?" she would say stoutly to defend herself. "That's right, Lois," he would say quietly.

When we were young, Irene and I decided that mother was the boss and Daddy had less influence on our lives. After we each married, we realized that Daddy had an inner strength that wasn't immediately apparent. One day we asked him why he did not argue with Mother if he felt she was wrong. "I like to keep the peace," he said quietly. As years passed, we saw that our father was living a Christlike life as few others do. He had a gentle spirit and loving manner that with few words eloquently reflected his Master's life and spirit.

When Daddy died, the year we moved to England, it was a sad time for me, because I felt I was just getting to know him and fully appreciate him. I felt I was learning more about the Christ life from him than from any other soul. I began to wish I had taken more heed of his words and actions. His prayers were simple and deep and full of the Spirit. How I wish I might have recorded at least one of them!

Now I was beginning to wonder, *What would my father say about Sue's astrology?* Would he barge in and want to put her straight in no uncertain terms, or would he look at her so gently as he used to do to me and smile lovingly, even when he may not have approved of my actions at the time? I was sure he would not be quick to give her his opinion. He'd let God speak to her Himself.

I thought again of that time in the lawyer's office, when I had to surrender tiny Sue to the nurse. And later, when in a vision I was surrendering her to Jesus. I began to think that Sue's love for astrology was not as important as my love for her and hers for me. Wasn't that enough? I wish I could say that I promptly concluded that I ought to suspend my arguments and let each of us hold our respective views. I knew that our relationship was more precious than winning a debate about astrology, and yet, at this point, I was not ready to give up quite so easily.

Not long afterward I watched a TV documentary about adoptive children and parents, showing how some relationships soured in an atmosphere of mistrust and argument. It reminded me how fragile any family relationship is, and one involved with adoption is even more delicate. I felt incredibly blessed that Sue and I were becoming so close in a truly loving relationship, despite those few differences.

CHAPTER TWENTY-FOUR

Tony's research at the university had provoked interest in numerous foreign students who wanted to study for their doctorates under his tutelage. Many Indian students were eager to work with him and he began to put into practice a conviction that had been growing since he became a professor. He saw how many foreign students gravitated to the US or UK to get higher degrees and then applied for jobs in the West where salaries far exceeded those in their home countries. He told me it was a sort of "reverse foreign aid" in which America and Britain profited handsomely; poorer foreign countries paid for their students' early education and first degrees, and then lost them—the investment in their education and any further expertise they had to share—to wealthier countries. The US and UK had not had to pay many thousands to educate these young men and women and were fortunate to skim the cream off the top of their lives.

Thus he began to study the economic needs of the various countries represented in his department, and he encouraged young Indians, Chinese, Poles, or Mexicans to take up projects that would aid their home countries. Very soon he saw these students eager to apply their knowledge to help their own people. Many who had plans to remain in the West were glad to return to their homes and profitable employment with national companies. In time the vast majority of foreign students who worked in his department did not remain in the West but caught the challenge to make a difference at home.

In connection with these postgraduate studies, Tony was eventually chosen to head a British aid project to India, where a number of his students were working on energy problems to benefit their country. And the year after Sue came back into my life, Tony found himself traveling to India to begin the program.

He was based at the National Chemical Laboratory in Poona (renamed Pune) and spent a month there on his first trip. He came home full of enthusiasm for the country, the people, his excellent and hardworking students, and the ancient culture that first captivated him at Oxford when he roomed next to a Maharajah's son. But he had never imagined spending time in that extraordinary subcontinent!

On his return home, Tony's enthusiasm convinced me that he'd better take me along the following year. We subsequently went through the complicated routine of inoculations and other requirements and the maddening bureaucracy of getting a visa from the Indian authorities. Months later we landed in Bombay (later renamed Mumbai), with dirt or macadam roads teeming constantly with bullocks, carts, festooned lorries with horns blaring, rickshaws, bicycles, and old Austins vying with a multitude of people of every description. It reminded me of the biblical picture of Jerusalem during Pentecost in Acts 2—the meeting place of men "from every nation under heaven" (v. 5). In villages especially, we felt as if we were being hurtled back in time a millennium or two.

But from the first week of my visit, I happened to meet up with Christians who had been born into the Muslim or Hindu faiths. I couldn't resist taking down their stories, even though I had no idea what to do with them. These remarkable men and women won my admiration for their courage in stepping outside their own very ancient culture, often at the cost of parental disapproval or even persecution.

At the end of the month I had gathered a list of a hundred men and women from all over India who might meet with me on my next trips to tell me their stories. And for the following decade I traveled to India almost every year, sometimes with Tony, sometimes alone, to meet those wonderful "strangers and pilgrims" who would become the subjects of my next three books.

When it first became clear that this was turning into a book (or books), as I made up my lists, I was very concerned about "the one that got away." The first year as we traveled in Bangalore, I had wanted to meet up with Colonel Matthews, the head of a Christian relief organization called the Evangelical Fellowship of India Commission on Relief (EFICOR). I arranged to meet him at a given time, but was kept waiting due to the unexpected arrival of an old friend of the colonel. His secretary whispered to me about it, "The visitor's grandfather was once a headhunter in northeast India near the Burmese border, and now this gentleman, two generations later, is a beloved doctor and theologian!" Soon the door opened, a short oriental looking gentleman passed in front of me, nodded, and was gone. And I was ushered into the colonel's office for my visit.

Back home in England, I couldn't stop thinking about the oriental-looking little man. I hadn't got his name and although I wrote to EFICOR several times, describing him, I received no reply. I felt strongly that his story should be in my book, but I had no other way of contacting him.

As I began to collect moving testimonies of Indian Christians, I mentioned this venture in a letter to a British missionary friend, Heather, who was living in Greece. She immediately wrote back, *You* must *get in touch with Dr. I. Ben Wati! His grandfather was a headhunter in Northeast India and he has been a much-loved evangelist and theologian since getting his doctorate in the USA. In fact, he was the best man when my parents married during their term in India!*

Heather gave me Dr. Ben Wati's address in Bangalore and I wrote him at once. He promptly replied, *I am planning to come to a convention in Staffordshire in two months and I would be delighted to visit you at your home.* My head was spinning from these extraordinary God incidents!

Two months later I was overjoyed to see that dear saint climb down from the train at Crewe Station and shake my hand. It became the start of a unique and lasting friendship that remained until his death thirty years later.

During the days Ben was in our home, he shared about his grandfather's life, how he had been converted through the work of American missionaries, and how this impacted the entire tribe to also commit their lives to Jesus Christ. In time Ben's father was educated at mission schools and became a teacher. Ben went further still and after gaining an honor's degree was given a scholarship to do postgraduate work at Wheaton College in Illinois.

But I was particularly impressed when he described a time in India in 1947 when students like Ben took up the cry "Quit India!" as Indian students and others demanded independence from Britain. Ben had given his life to the Lord years earlier and was eager to commit his life's work to Jesus Christ. But then as a university student he seemed to get swept along in the enthusiasm of fighting for Indian "freedom" and it began to take more and more of his time. Gradually he became uneasy about what was happening to him.

Ben asked himself, "Am I an Indian first or am I a Christian first?" And even as he asked himself this question he felt he knew the answer. If he committed his whole life to Jesus Christ, any political issues had to take a backseat. He felt that his devotion had to be to the Lord, and he ought not to be sidetracked by any other issues. Real freedom, for Ben, came the night he discovered this. And he went on to be one of the most effective Indians for Christ in the past century.

I thought of Ben's response last year in Florida as I was waiting at the traffic lights behind a big new car. It had a large political slogan on the back, a picture of a gun, and (almost too small to notice) a Christian fish. I wondered what that fellow's priority was. A few days later I spied a truck with a huge banner on the back window—*Impeach Obama*—and a small cross on the bumper. Ben might have asked those fellows, "Are you a Christian first or a Republican first?"

Over the years as I returned to America from my home in England, I could see, almost as an outsider, that political allegiance in the US sometimes jars with the words of Jesus and what He asks of us. Jesus was no coward nor was he afraid to state publicly what He felt was wrong. He told those religious leaders that they were of their father the devil. I don't think He could have been more frank than that. But He also said, "My kingdom is not of this world. If My kingdom were of this world, My servants would fight" (John 18:36). How did that, I wondered, square with the American Christians, many of whom think it is their right to own as many guns as they wish and often support wars which are discovered later to be started on false premises?

Having lived in the UK for more years than in my own country, I have been able to take a more international view. I'm neither anti-American nor un-American. I will always be an American living in England and proud of it. But my first priority is to live as a servant of Jesus Christ. Everything else is secondary.

I was interested in the phrase "What would Jesus do?" when it first became popular. I couldn't imagine Him standing on a street corner with a sign declaring *God hates gays*—a sight I have seen numerous times, with passionate evangelicals wanting the world to know what God hates. I know God hates sin, but He loves the sinner. I know God hates hypocrisy and lack of love. Many Scriptures tell us that if we do not love, we do not know God! Those are hard words to receive!

Indian Christians have taught me many things over the years. One extraordinary conversation I remember was about the difficulties Christians faced in a staunch Hindu culture. There was an election in one part of India where the choice was between a moderate Hindu candidate and an extreme fundamentalist Hindu. My Christian friend believed that the best choice for Christians was to vote for the fundamentalist Hindu. "Why?" I asked him. He said that Christians are stronger for the Lord in times of persecution than when they are merely tolerated. He cited many examples throughout history to support this view.

In the coming decades, I was amazed to think how Tony's university projects propelled us into Hindu India where we met so many of God's people from all walks of life. Some, like Ben Wati, had public ministries and their witnesses inspired multitudes. Others included impoverished villagers and homeless people who are invisible to the masses but who nevertheless believe devoutly in Jesus Christ and are living for a kingdom "not of this world." Some day they will be given choice seats of honor in the heavenly kingdom.

As a result of what I saw in India and in other countries, I knew I had to live as a "Christian first and American second." Ben Wati helped me keep the right perspective.

Those annual trips to India in the 1980s created extraordinary memories for me. To think of Vera Weiss from Liberty

Street, standing before the Taj Mahal, or being held aloft in a sedan chair, carried by four spindly legged Indians up the side of a mountain! Sometimes Tony indulged me in shopping for a few silk carpets, or gold embroidered saris, or an emerald ring, or jade or ivory beads. But by far our most memorable treasures are the bonds we forged with doctors and pastors, charity workers, businessmen and housewives, the poorest of the poor, all one in Christ Jesus although coming out from a variety of religions to face rejection and persecution in the service of their Lord! Those are my most invaluable memories.

CHAPTER TWENTY-FIVE

M y niece Susan and her husband had their first child in January 1985, a miracle baby named Tyler. It was an anxious time for the family as he was a premie and weighed less than three pounds at birth. Thankfully he thrived and was later followed by two beautiful sisters with their mother's blonde coloring. It was the experience of giving birth that made Susan think seriously for the first time about her birth mother. What was she like? What would she think of her grandchildren? Where does she live? Above all, does she know the Lord? This curiosity was kindled by a new generation of TV dramas and documentaries about adoption and about the reactions of mothers and children to the more relaxed procedures permitting reunions between them.

Susan knew that the subject of adoption was a sticky one with my sister. Irene had proudly shown us a scrapbook she made for the children when they were around five years of age, with pictures and captions pasted around the heading of "Adoption"— showing how adopted children are special and extra loved. But after using the scrapbook as bedtime reading for a brief period, Irene tucked the book away and it was never referred to again. Through her growing up years, Susan learned that it was not a subject that Irene appreciated.

When a close friend in the church asked for details about

her children's adoption, Irene got so angry that her friend was shocked at her reaction. And when a single mother came to the church with her child, Irene let it be known that she did not approve of the general wave of acceptance for the newcomer. All these incidents confirmed to Susan that it was a subject that would not be welcome in Irene's presence. She would never be able to confide in Irene about this. Nevertheless, she found herself thinking more and more of the possibility of finding her birth mother. With Brad's help and blessing, she began to inquire of various agencies how to go about this.

At the same time Susan and I entered into a new email relationship, and I told her about the wonderful correspondence I was enjoying with "my Sue." It gave my niece a fresh perspective toward her Aunt Vicki whom she had always been told had sinned greatly and was apparently still out of favor. In fact, Irene claimed to Susan that the cause of my mother's deafness was due directly to the shock of learning of my sin back in 1955. She told her daughter that I was her "greatest disappointment."

I had to put my relationship with Irene on the back burner, as it distressed me if I gave it much thought. In fact, I asked a Christian psychologist what I should do about it. "Distance yourself emotionally from her" was his advice, and I decided to follow that suggestion for the time being.

Meanwhile life was good for Tony and me at Copperfield. As we entered the late 1980s, we lived comfortably and surrounded ourselves with professional people at the university and Christian couples from our church and other churches nearby. We were perhaps a bit too ambitious for our sons to achieve academic success. And I will admit I wanted Tony to reap the rewards of his hard work and dedication at the university. He always seemed to be studying and writing articles and textbooks. When he wasn't doing that, he was devoting himself to the study and editing of PhD theses, a growing pile of which sat in the corner of our library. Other professors had a way of elbowing their way to this or that award, but Tony just kept his head down and preferred to help others in the department to succeed rather than himself.

But ambition can be an insidious emotion, one which can be justified by Scripture verses as well as self-help books. The successes or achievements we quietly coveted for ourselves or our children would, we believed, aid in our spiritual growth and were ways in which we might better serve God. Years later I looked back at that time and decided we were fooling ourselves. We were being gently led back into the world's orbit by an inconspicuous greed for greater comfort or approval. We could see other Christians achieving financial reward for themselves or academic success for their children. Silently it grieved us that such "blessings" eluded us. Why, we wondered! Was this a tiny "root of bitterness" that only God could see?

Yet still we praised God, believed Him absolutely, loved Him completely. We read the Scriptures in bed on rising each morning and prayed faithfully. We felt we would have given our lives rather than deny the faith. So we continued all the godly pursuits that showed us to be passionate about Jesus—evangelical, charismatic believers who constantly asked God to fill us, mold us, and use us. We believed we meant this with all our hearts.

That was the year our boys both moved to London to pursue their careers and we found ourselves in a house too large for our purposes. It was the year that Tony was offered a sabbatical at the University of Kansas and it confirmed our conviction that it was time to sell Copperfield rather than close it up and come back to an overgrown garden the following year. We found a beautiful new apartment nearby which was on the ground floor, opening onto our own small private garden.

We were in Blackpool that spring, attending the annual Full Gospel Businessmen's convention, when Tony suffered a heart attack. It threw all our neatly organized plans out the window. Tony wound up in Blackpool Hospital, praying that the Lord would spare him, like Hezekiah, for fifteen more years. And when he was well enough to go home, there was still uncertainty about the year in Kansas. Would he be well enough by August to travel?

In the midst of such life-threatening news, all our former petty longings were forgotten. We were on our knees now, begging God for Tony's life, but also, I'll admit, a resumption of our trouble-free and comfortable existence. We still weren't listening fully. Finally, in late summer, the doctors discharged Tony and said he was fit to travel. We closed up our new apartment and flew to the USA, feeling like honeymooners. A new start!

We had been told that accommodations would be supplied, but we didn't have any details. As we touched down in Kansas City, this verse suddenly came to mind: "The rain is over and gone . . . The time of singing of birds has come" (Song 2:11–12).

We were met at the airport by my cousin Dr. Bill Harley and his wife, Joyce, who took a long detour through other states to pick us up and drive us to our new address in Lawrence, Kansas. They even took us to our first-ever professional baseball game in the Kansas City stadium. That night we arrived in Lawrence to find that our temporary abode was a beautiful, spacious, and modern four-bedroom home, fully furnished and supplied with everything we could possibly need. We went through room after room, praising God for supplying our needs "more than we could ask or think."

And amongst the letters awaiting us was a card from my favorite King's College professor Dr. Dorothy Braun with a verse on the cover:

Rise up, my love, my fair one, and come away
for lo, the winter is past, the rain is over and gone;
the time of the singing of birds is come . . ."
(Song 2:10-12)

What a clear message from the Lord to assure us of His direction and protection as we entered this new phase of our lives. Yes, we gave thanks for the break from the rainy winter season in Britain, and now we enjoyed the large windows in our new home that overlooked lush trees filled with singing birds of every description. We both wept to realize God's love and protection and provision in bringing Tony back from a near fatal illness and, above all, reviving our spirits. It was a year of refreshing that caught us totally off guard. God came down and so unexpectedly brought revival to our souls. Until then we had not known how badly we needed Him to do this!

We enjoyed worshiping in a variety of churches in Lawrence that year—from magnificent structures like the First Presbyterian Church, to an on-campus meeting place with local Mennonites, and a small Indian Baptist Church across town where we were privileged to meet many Native American Christians. This started me on another quest to interview a variety of Native Americans about their faith.

That first night in the Indian Baptist Church we sat in the last row, two white faces amidst the fifty Native Americans who all turned around and stared at us. It made us aware of how minority people feel in a reverse situation. We followed their songs in the hymnal, many of which I knew from my Mennonite childhood. But some were unfamiliar, with melodies in a minor key, a distinctive Indian feature. One especially brought tears to my eyes: a plaintive cry to the Lord for protection and deliverance in the face of evil. A footnote on the page said: "This hymn was written during the Trail of Tears in 1860, when twenty-five percent of the men, women, and children died of cold or starvation on the forced march from the East Coast to their new reservation lands in Oklahoma."

It made me weep all the more. People just like those dear folks sitting all around us, hounded or tricked out of their national homelands, into the so-called "protection" of the American authorities! I had studied American history from the time I was six years old right through graduate school, but no one ever taught us about the Trail of Tears. I was determined to learn more.

That night there was an impassioned sermon by Rev. Cloyd Harjo after which an old-fashioned altar call was made as the small congregation sang an invitational hymn. A number of men and women moved to the front and knelt at the altar, some unashamedly weeping. Afterward many people came to us and shyly greeted us. Rev. Harjo welcomed us and hoped we'd come again. I was determined to do so.

During that remarkable year at the University of Kansas, we were privileged to attend memorable concerts including one featuring the famous cellist Yo-Yo Ma and another featuring KU composer John Pozdro's fine work. John and his wife, Shirley, were devout Christians who became dear friends from that year on. We were so blessed to meet many great people within the university and local churches. And weekly I joined a group of professors' wives for a morning Bible study. We took turns hosting sessions in each of our kitchens, sitting around the table with our Bibles and coffee cups.

We even enjoyed a family reunion with Weiss cousins from Kansas, Missouri, and Pennsylvania as they converged on our temporary home. They stayed for a long weekend and we were glad we could accommodate them all in our three spacious guest suites. We spent many happy hours talking and praying together, discussing the precious heritage we enjoyed from godly ancestors. This rare opportunity seeing cousins Grace, Beatrice, Alvin, and his wife, Vicki, all seemed to be part of God's special gift of healing for both Tony and me.

At the close of those blessed nine months, before heading back to England, we allowed ourselves one final extravagant treat—a trip to Hawaii. We first flew to California, to visit my beloved aunt and uncle Will and Rita Harley and cousins Jim and Jan Harley Brown. Then off to Oahu and Kauai for the perfect ending to an extraordinary year.

But above all the wonderful experiences, trips and the Christian friendships forged in that beautiful midwestern state, we had our spiritual batteries recharged through a new touch from our blessed Lord.

I did not forget my determination to learn more about Native American history and the seed of an idea was formed through my study. I resolved to return to Kansas the following year after collecting names and addresses of Native Americans from a variety of tribes who were willing to be interviewed at that time.

Because email was not as common at that time, it was necessary to write airmail letters which could take a week to travel across the Atlantic and at least another week to await the reply.

Eventually, I collected several dozen names of Native Americans willing to speak with me about their Christian faith. These were from a dozen or more tribes, some on reservations and others living in the general population in Kansas, Oklahoma, and Nebraska. I couldn't wait to be with them all the following year.

Meanwhile I planned my own course of study of the trials and tribulations suffered by Native Americans in times past. I began to learn the bitter truths about Presidents Thomas Jefferson, Andrew Jackson, John Quincy Adams, and Martin Van Buren and their systematic efforts to weaken and even destroy the natives so that settlers could take their lands. Thomas Jefferson may be known largely as the writer of the Declaration of Independence and the lofty words "all men are created equal" but I was only now learning about his lesser-known and sinister plans for the natives who were obviously not created equal.

It was Jefferson who devised an "Indian solution," a plan that was taken up by successive presidents to remove the natives from their fertile lands and drive them into inhospitable areas to the west. This caused the deaths of thousands of men, women, and children from the eastern coastal areas as they trekked in bitter winter weather to reservations in Oklahoma. The plains Indians were endangered in another way. Their culture was dependent on the buffalo for food, housing, clothing, and even tools. They were to see the buffalo systematically killed as the government's way of weakening and destroying the tribes there.

I was disturbed at the reactions of many educated Americans to this information. Many refused to believe such "anti-American propaganda." Many were offended at the "criticism" of early presidents. Some felt that modern American Indians had it easy with plenty of welfare so that they didn't need to work. Others pointed out the few tribes who were made wealthy in recent years with the success of casinos. No one seemed bothered by the fact that we had been raised on a sanitized version of Native American history. We learned as youngsters about the wicked Indians who attacked settlers and scalped them. Movies used this theme for decades and American youngsters were fed a steady diet of cowboys and Indians in which the "savages" menaced and tortured the good settlers and courageous cowboys. But there had been a serious flaw in our modern education when little or nothing was taught of the deceitful and murderous schemes made by successive presidents in an effort to solve the "Indian problem."

In subsequent years I learned much from my time spent with Indian Christian men and women. It was a sad revelation. I found that many tribespeople were and are demoralized and discouraged, often depending on alcohol and drugs to cope with their sad history and their life in the land that has been taken from them. And yet there are also fine Christians who have been converted from addiction and despair and are now faithfully proclaiming a new and powerful life in Jesus Christ. These are our brothers and sisters, and they are an addition to the body of Christ that we should treasure.

CHAPTER TWENTY-SIX

In the years after Sue and I had our life-changing reunion, we enjoyed yearly visits back and forth. Sue sometimes flew to England to spend a few weeks with my family at Copperfield, and other times I visited her at her home in the USA. My first visit to her was in 1986 when she was doing graduate work at the University of New Orleans and also working as a teaching assistant there. I was there during my birthday, and as a surprise, she and her partner took me on a paddle steamer on the Mississippi. We enjoyed Sunday brunch with a jazz quartet playing appropriate music for the jazz capital.

Later Sue moved to Los Angeles and took up a position in the space industry. It gave me great opportunities to be together in the state I've always favored. On one visit Sue planned a special birthday treat for us to ride in a hot air balloon over the California mountains and briefly out over the Pacific. The following year I surprised her with a helicopter ride over the Grand Canyon, touching down for breakfast on an Arizona ranch, serenaded by cowboys as we ate. On one visit I climbed on the back of Sue's motorcycle and we joined twenty thousand bikers and their partners roaring up Route 5 for that year's Love Ride in aid of the Muscular Dystrophy charity. On this hundred-mile journey we enjoyed a day at Castaic Lake, watching a parachute display and other features.

A year or two later we met up in Las Vegas and enjoyed a week in that crazy, glittering city. I'm sure we had far more fun people-watching than others who lost thousands of dollars gambling. A year later we both flew in to Pennsylvania and spent the week together traveling throughout the Amish and Mennonite communities, staying in bed and breakfasts on farms or in the small towns. We enjoyed worshiping in a Mennonite Church together one Sunday. We left an afternoon free to travel back in time to Allentown, the city of our births, to see how our small hometown had changed, compared to our youthful memories of it.

That year I arrived in Pennsylvania a few days earlier, to visit with my dearest Ruth Schwenk, staying in her parents' Schuylkill Haven house that I remembered from my childhood. I had not seen Ruth for more than a decade, and it was a very emotional reunion for both of us. She was, as always, simply dwelling in Christ, simply yet powerfully so. But there was such joy in her presence. And her laughter was so infectious that I always longed to just sit at her feet and learn from her. Even though years went by without seeing each other, we knew God had put us together for a very special reason. I came away from those visits a bit closer to my Lord and Savior.

After thirty years as professor and head of the chemical engineering department at the University of Salford, Tony retired. The previous year, he had been awarded the DSc in a moving ceremony in which Prince Philip presented him with his degree. This, his second doctorate, was awarded for his work in renewable energy projects in both India and Mexico. The projects that had been so successful in India were lately being taken up by the University of Morelos in Cuernavaca, Mexico, and after Tony's retirement he was asked to spend long periods in Mexico working with the graduate students there.

The unique project he devised was called the "en casa" program because he was bringing Salford University to their own home surroundings, allowing them to continue working and studying on their own soil. In time he devised a schedule of spending eight weeks in Mexico, three times a year. Then we thought "commuting" would be far easier if we purchased a small house in the USA near the Mexican border. We looked in both San Antonio, Texas, and communities in Florida, finally selecting a plot of land in a golf-course community north of Tampa, where three of my cousins had settled.

Thus I began to spend the winter months in Florida while Tony worked in Mexico. He'd return to Tampa for a few months before heading back to Mexico. He loved the work and felt privileged to be able to be of use. And the university had recently invited him to become a professor in the chemical engineering department there, which he accepted.

Although I felt privileged to be able to spend almost half of each year with my cousins and their mates, communication with Irene had not resumed. She sometimes sent a letter describing vacations abroad, but there seemed little opportunity for dialogue and I felt cut off from her completely.

But her daughter, Susan, and I had maintained loving links and I enjoyed hearing about Brad's work as a United Airlines pilot, their three growing children, and their activities at their local church. Susan began to ask me questions about how I found my daughter or how she found me. She wrote that for several years she had quietly tried to seek her birth mother but that so far she was unsuccessful. She knew that if she ever found her, it would be a huge problem telling Irene about it.

And then suddenly, she learned where her birth mother lived; and best of all, she was willing to meet Susan. Susan was overjoyed, but also apprehensive. On a monumental day I knew only too well, she and Brad went to New Jersey to meet Hedy and her husband, Wolf. It was a loving meeting between the two couples, and Susan and Hedy arranged to meet again soon. She learned that her mother had not had other children, and she looked forward to building a close relationship with the older woman and to learning more about her heritage.

On their return home, Susan and Brad spoke of the next big event—telling Irene and Don what she had done. It was a nerve-wracking time for Susan who knew she could be bringing down upon herself a torrent when Irene learned what had just taken place. After months of anguish and prayer, Susan sat down and wrote a loving letter to Irene, explaining what a wonderful mother Irene was and how grateful she was for her upbringing. But knowing she was adopted, it created many questions about the family she came from, their health issues and background—so many details that other children know from their earliest years. She hastened to assure Irene that she would always be her mother, and no one would ever take her place. But finally, she explained that she had searched through various agencies, that she had at last found her birth mother—a German-born woman who married late and had no other children—and that she had gone to see her.

To no one's surprise, the reaction was explosive and angry. "Did Vicki put you up to this?" was one of Irene's first comments. And although Susan pleaded with her to understand and respect her decision, Irene remained furious and unforgiving. She cut off all contact and did not see Susan again for almost ten years.

CHAPTER TWENTY-SEVEN

After three decades of living in England, it was a rare treat to have a base back in my native country. Tony and I began worshiping in the local church in central Florida and visiting with neighbors in our community. We purchased a new Chrysler and started to explore the area. We loved returning to life in America, which reminded us of those carefree days we enjoyed as a young newly married couple in New Jersey thirty years earlier.

But whereas we had worshiped in Plymouth Brethren chapels in our early years of marriage, our first years in England were spent with the Baptists, then in a charismatic Christian fellowship for twenty years. As we got older, the guitar music seemed to get louder. Although we were enriched by the Bible study and worship in that church, we began to long to return to the old hymns of the faith—something more traditional. I was as surprised as the next person the morning I walked across the road from our apartment in Bowdon, to the local Church of England. And I immediately felt at home.

The first time I stepped into All Saints Episcopal Church in Scarborough, New York, all those years before, I knew that God had directed me there. It was just a brief interlude, because after Tony and I married we settled into the Plymouth Brethren chapel near our home. Now many years later I was returning to the Anglican worship, and I felt much enriched by it.

Since we were spending more time in Florida, too, we sought out the local Episcopal church and immediately felt a part of that. But trouble was brewing within the Episcopal Church in the United States of America (ECUSA) hierarchy, and during the next few years a more liberal approach to many issues caused severe divisions within the Episcopal church.

Many conservative Episcopalians throughout the USA decided to leave, often at great personal loss as the churches they had supported faithfully for many years now reverted to the Diocese. Some preferred to give up these valuable properties and be homeless for a time rather than continue their allegiance to a hierarchy that was denying central tenets in the Scriptures. It became a distressing time for many of my Episcopal friends who were torn between the familiarity and comfort and fellowship of the local Episcopal church community and an uncertain future as Anglicans-at-large.

Back in England, I found new pleasure in worshiping at the local Church of England. I wasn't fooled into thinking that it was a perfect church. If conservative Episcopalians in the USA thought that bypassing ECUSA and becoming "American Anglicans" solved their problems, they were looking at the Church of England through rose-colored glasses. There were political issues causing disagreement and concern on that side of the Atlantic too.

When a new Archbishop of Canterbury was elected, conservatives were disappointed. It was, it seemed, just another political appointment sanctioned by a small but powerful clique. Those bishops that were most forthright in wanting to spread the gospel of Jesus Christ were overlooked, although a few we most earnestly prayed for came close to being nominated. In the end, we couldn't say it was God's choice.

But what church was perfect? Often it seemed that the most sacrificial and energetic Christians were those quietly living their godly lives without fanfare or recognition. God knew who they were. And although some of my evangelical friends seemed disappointed that we had moved to the Anglicans, I knew it was in one's personal daily encounters with the Lord Jesus Christ that a believer either grows or loses ground.

While I never believed one had to become a member of a church to develop one's spiritual potential, I suddenly felt the urge to be officially a part of that extraordinary community called the Church of England. It meant being confirmed, and I was willing to go through this ceremony as another step of obedience to my Lord and Master. In the traditional Anglican view, a baby is christened and thus becomes a member of the church of Jesus Christ. Then, perhaps around age twelve or thirteen, he or she is encouraged to go through confirmation classes to confirm the commitment made by his parents at his christening. It is believed that the Holy Spirit comes upon the young person at this time.

I did not hesitate to make it clear to my vicar that I disagreed with some of these traditions. First of all, I did not believe that a child becomes a member of God's family merely by being christened. Particularly since so many British couples seemed to use this event as a social experience rather than a spiritual one. And if a young person is urged to be confirmed because his or her friends are doing it, then the value is lost and it becomes a hollow ceremony. I knew I had already accepted Christ into my life and that the Holy Spirit had already indwelt me. I knew I was already a child of God, not by my own merit, but because the Lord Jesus took upon Himself my sins on His own body at Calvary.

My vicar, Bernard, was a very tolerant fellow and smiled and agreed that it was perfectly all right that I felt this way, and he gladly decided to approve my application without any need for confirmation classes. That summer Tony and I and a number of our friends traveled to the county seat of Chester, that wonderful medieval city with the thousand-year-old church standing proudly beside the Roman walls, and I was privileged to be confirmed and blessed by Bishop Peter together with a few dozen other confirmants.

I was especially blessed by partaking of the Eucharist that afternoon, remembering my Lord's command to "do this in remembrance of Me" (Luke 22:19). My eyes were moist as I repeated the Prayer of Humble Access:

> We do not presume to come to this Thy table, O merciful Lord, trusting in our own righteousness but in Thy manifold and great mercies. We are not worthy so much as to gather up the crumbs under Thy table. But Thou art the same Lord whose property is always to have mercy: Grant us therefore, gracious Lord, so to eat the flesh of Thy dear Son Jesus Christ and to drink His blood, that our sinful bodies may be made clean by His body and our souls washed through His most precious blood, and that we may evermore dwell in Him, and He in us. Amen.

CHAPTER TWENTY-EIGHT

One summer's day when Jon and Paula's children, Charlotte and Aaron, were just four and six years old, I entertained them with a story. We sat around the dining room table at Beech Lawn, and little Charlotte's head just barely rose above the table, but her wide eyes showed she was taking in every word of the Bible story. It was the account of Jesus gathering the little children around Him and blessing them. The disciples felt that they should move on, so that Jesus could teach the adults in the crowd. But Jesus told the disciples that those children were as important as any adult and that, in fact, people could only enter the kingdom of heaven if they had the faith of a little child.

I asked Charlotte and Aaron how they thought anyone got to heaven. This led to the verse where Jesus said that He stood at the door and knocked, and that He was willing to come in to anyone's heart if they opened the door to Him. We discussed this and then I asked Aaron if he might like to ask Jesus into his heart. He agreed and I was pleased to pray with him as he took this first important step. Afterward Charlotte looked up at me and asked, "Why can't *I* ask Jesus to come into *my* heart?" And so we prayed for her too. I felt that a significant step had been taken by each of my grandchildren, and I considered it a very important and wonderful day.

Aaron usually visited his other grandparents on weekends, and as Charlotte grew, she wanted to regularly visit her Holland grandparents. Tony and I loved having her with us, and sometimes we took her to Yorkshire, where she enjoyed staying in the little room under the eaves overlooking the Yorkshire Mountains.

In years to come, when Tony was working abroad, I loved to take Charlotte further afield, to visit the birthplaces of writers whose books she began to read. We spent some time in Brontë country, in Yorkshire, and read books together by the Brontë sisters. We visited Shakespeare's birthplace, and she learned a bit about that great writer. Later we took a special trip to Amsterdam, and toured Anne Frank's house. She loved reading the diary of Anne Frank, and even wrote a poem about her, which was published on the Anne Frank website.

Most of all, Charlotte began to read and enjoy many Bible stories from both the Old and New Testaments in her children's Bible. She had a remarkable ability to retain many details about the Bible characters: prophets, priests, kings, and especially about the Lord Jesus. We had fun devising a Bible Alphabet Quiz, where she answered questions about more than one hundred characters and even from the age of five learned how to spell correctly many of their names.

She represented to me the little daughter I was unable to raise. She had a very special place in my heart.

As Tony and I approached the fortieth anniversary of our marriage in 1998, I thought how good it would be to take a special European tour to celebrate the occasion. I suggested flying from Manchester to Paris, where we would spend a few days in that magical city. We could then board the Eurostar train to Lake Lucerne to spend three days there, then on to Florence to tour that ancient city for five days. For our last stop we could take the train to Monaco and spend three days in that tiny kingdom. Our final journey would take us back to Paris and home.

Conservative Tony frowned at first—oh, the expense! But in the end he realized what a wonderful trip it could be, and he agreed. As things worked out, I have cherished the memory of that trip over all our vacations.

CHAPTER TWENTY-NINE

By 1999, we had settled into an easy arrangement traveling between the two countries. And Tony, traveling between three. Christmas in Florida was always a novelty: Christmas lights on palm trees was not something I ever expected to see. Our small corner of Florida called Beverly Hills always attracted volunteers to put up thousands of lights around Lake Beverly—a staggering sight.

Then two days after Christmas, I drove Tony back to Tampa airport for his flight to Mexico. He planned to remain there until March after which we would fly back to England together. But I was concerned about the pain in his right side that he had struggled with all during Christmas week. We even went to a walk-in clinic two days before Christmas, but the doctor thought it might be kidney stones. Tony assured me that the medical service was excellent in Cuernavaca, and should he need any further advice or medication, he was in good hands.

Thus began a continual flow of faxes back and forth as Tony reported about his continuing pain, the various doctors who examined him, the tests they gave him, the medication recommended. When these things didn't ease the pain, they thought he should be on a strict diet. Later they decided he needed special injections every other day. All the while he continued to work a heavy schedule of appointments and tutoring with the graduate students involved with the "en casa" program.

One fax told me he was back in the Cuernavaca Hospital. *I have had the most excellent round-the-clock medical care and a very thorough diagnosis at a fraction of what it would cost in the USA. I have many visitors from the university, and I try to keep up with the work from my bedside. But I hope they will release me in a day or two.*

The next fax said: *I am spending a good deal of time reading the Bible. I should have returned to work at the university today but the specialist who I saw on Saturday said not to return until February 24. I was able to send for additional books from my office and now I can more easily work in my room.*

Although the medical team says they know what is causing the pain, they say it will take some time to cure. I am very well looked after, but above all, I know the Lord is looking after me.

The next fax reported: *I have had to return to the hospital for a laparoscopy but was released today. The good news was that they didn't find anything but some adhesions which they separated. I am completely free from lumps of any kind and I have no cancer. The treatment has been excellent and of little cost, but the medications here are very expensive. This is something I had not bargained for and it has really hit me in the pocket. However I am trusting the Lord to take care of us.*

I drove to Tampa Airport the following week to pick him up. I longed for him to have a restful, quiet time in the little villa he loved so much. I prayed he would be free of pain and that somehow, someone could find out what the problem was. I wasn't so sure that he had had the correct diagnosis there, despite all their best efforts, because whatever was attempted, he still experienced pain beneath his right rib.

It was a shock to see him enter through customs and walk slowly toward me. He held out his arms and I fell into them.

He seemed to have lost a great deal of weight in the ten weeks since he left. His face was so gaunt that I wondered whether it wouldn't be better to fly home rather than wait it out in Florida. I didn't want him to go through more painful tests, and I felt sure he needed to get back to England to find the answers that still eluded us.

He insisted that he wanted to keep to the schedule and have a final two weeks in Florida, so life suddenly slowed down and we went out when he felt able, and we sat by the swimming pool in the sunshine, and we went once or twice to a few of his favorite restaurants, although he ate very little. I was conscious of the clock ticking, and I looked forward to our flight and the return home.

The day after arriving back in England, we arranged an immediate private appointment with a consultant. He told us later that before doing any tests, he sensed it was cancer of the lung. "It was a particularly difficult form to identify," he explained. "It wasn't in a firm lump but it was a spongy substance. This type of lung cancer doesn't always show up in X rays."

The pain continued, and it was recommended that he have a procedure to deaden the nerve on his right side. Even that operation didn't reduce the pain. Tony was later advised by an oncologist to begin chemotherapy. We talked it over and decided to decline it, since the doctor didn't think he would survive for more than eighteen months even with the treatment. "Why suffer with chemo just to prolong the pain a few more months?" he said. I agreed, for his sake. On Good Friday we were told they could do nothing more apart from heavy pain medication and we went home together for the last time. I slipped away while he was sleeping and attended the Good Friday service across the road. But I did not find much comfort there, and on the verge of tears, I rushed out early to stay with him in our room.

Our local doctor kept showing up at our door, even when we didn't ask him to. "If he keeps on coming like this, we'll have to give him his own key!" Tony joked at one point. Our doctor knew that Tony didn't want to have his suffering prolonged, since he had told the doctor that he was ready to meet the Lord at any time. And so he gave us a morphine pump which either Tony or I could pump as needed.

Tony became so drowsy from the diamorphine that often he would fall asleep as he was putting a cup of tea to his lips, and I had to catch the cup before it fell. He was his old gentle, sweet self, so grateful for my help and ministrations. "Whatever would I do without you?" he'd say, softly, lovingly.

I would cry and respond, "I wouldn't be anywhere else in the world but here with you!" Despite what was happening to him, life was very precious to both of us. God was filling us with His peace in the midst of our sorrow.

In his final weeks, Tony remained in bed, too full of drugs to stay awake, but free from former pain. The final weekend I could no longer lift him, and our doctor said it was time to take him to the nearby St. Anne's Hospice, a beautiful place that had a room all ready for him. I didn't wait for an ambulance but just carried his thin frame to a wheelchair, wheeled it to the car, and then lifted him into the seat. He looked back without comment at the handsome Edwardian building that had been his happy home for thirteen years. I was thinking of his prayer that he might have another fifteen years, like Hezekiah, after his heart attack in 1987. I wondered whether he was thinking that too.

We drove up to St. Anne's Hospice which is surrounded by beautiful trees and landscaping. A worker rushed out and lifted him carefully into a wheelchair. When he was settled into his bed, the doctor came to greet him and ask him a few questions. "And do you have faith, Professor?" he asked him.

At once Tony revived and smiled a gaunt smile. "Oh yes!" he said. "I believe in the Lord Jesus Christ, and I am about to meet Him!"

The nurse standing by came to me and said, "My husband is the chaplain here, and he would be glad to give you and your husband Holy Communion if you like."

"Oh yes, we would love that," I said. And soon the room emptied of workers, and the chaplain and his wife stood with us as we took Holy Communion.

> We do not presume to come to this Thy table, O merciful Lord, trusting in our own righteousness, but in Thy manifold and great mercies . . . we are not worthy so much as to gather the crumbs from under Thy table . . . But Thou art the same Lord, whose property is always to have mercy . . .

Jon stayed with Tony that night, sleeping beside him in a chair, while I got some much needed sleep at home. When I returned the next morning, Tony had slipped into a coma. Chris brought his wife, Carol, and three-year-old son, Thomas, to say good-bye, and the boy climbed over the bed, not realizing what was happening to his Pop-Pop. Tony's sister, Margaret, arrived too. We spoke quietly together, but I was concerned that perhaps he could hear our trivial conversation.

After they left, I squeezed his hand. "You know I love you, don't you? If you do, squeeze my hand." And faintly I felt his fingers press against mine.

I then quietly sang to him the hymn "I Would Love to Tell You What I Think of Jesus." That was his favorite hymn since that weekend when we had first met. Now I sang it for him a final time. And then I whispered to him, "I wouldn't be anywhere else in the world except here with you!" How can I describe how precious those moments were?

Jon and I remained with Tony one more night. My dearest husband died just after midnight, July 10, 2000.

With my other Sue, 2007

SUSAN

Newlyweds Owen and Jayne Lowery, 2013

Tommy on death row, 1988

Thirty-nine years on death row, 2015

That following weekend in July of 2000, the bells of St. Margaret's Church rang in solemn tones to invite friends and family to Tony's funeral. Since I lived just across the main road from the church, it wasn't necessary to have a limo driving the family to the service. Not only did my sons and their families join me in walking across the road, my many Jewish neighbors at Beech Lawn honored Tony by attending the funeral too. We made quite a sight as we stopped traffic on our way across the busy street to the church.

The casket was followed down the center aisle by our family as the organist played Bach's "Jesu, Joy of Man's Desiring," one of our favorite hymns. Six-year-old Charlotte and eight-year-old Aaron, Jon and Paula's children, stood beneath the pulpit and read passages from the Psalms clearly and beautifully. Our longtime friend Roger Stanway read the gospel lesson, and I chose to read the passage from St. Paul's second letter to the Corinthians, chapter 4, which defined my thoughts and prayers at this time:

> For it is the God who commanded light to shine out of darkness, who has shone in our hearts to give the light of the knowledge of the glory of God in the face of Jesus Christ.

But we have this treasure in earthen vessels, that the excellence of the power may be of God and not of us. We are hard-pressed on every side, yet not crushed; we are perplexed, but not in despair; persecuted, but not forsaken; struck down, but not destroyed—always carrying about in the body the dying of the Lord Jesus, that the life of Jesus also may be manifested in our body. For we who live are always delivered to death for Jesus' sake, that the life of Jesus also may be manifested in our mortal flesh. So then death is working in us, but life in you.

And as the service came to a close, the *Nunc dimittis*:

Lord, now lettest Thou Thy servant depart in peace: according to Thy word . . . For mine eyes have seen Thy salvation, which thou hast prepared before the face of all people, to be a light to lighten the Gentiles and to be the glory of Thy people Israel.

It had only been a few months since we learned of Tony's cancer, and suddenly he was gone. He was a wonderful, faithful companion for forty-two years, and I was blessed indeed to have loved and been loved by this great man. Above all, he was a true Christian gentleman, without guile.

But I had depended on him far more than I realized, with car repairs, tax issues, insurance forms, and all other financial matters. I assumed all those years that I was a pretty independent woman, but now I sensed that so much of our life together was carefully organized by him, and I was totally ignorant of such details.

Now I wondered whether I could afford to continue living as before; would I manage to keep on top of bills and taxes, repairs and decoration to two homes, and the upkeep of two cars? And increasingly expensive trans-Atlantic flights?

During the days after Tony's death, I was overwhelmed with peace from the Lord. Some friends were concerned and assured me that this wouldn't last, that it would hit me after a brief respite. But I was learning to trust the Lord more than ever before, and God had begun to teach me about this new life that He had permitted, which would draw me closer to Him than at any other time in my life. I was directed back to that amazing chapter in Isaiah 54 that had spoken to me so clearly that morning of Sue's phone call in 1984. This time, I saw something there that I had not seen previously:

Fear not . . . for thy Maker is thine husband;
the LORD of hosts is his name;
and thy Redeemer the Holy One of Israel.
　(Isa. 54:4–5 KJV)

It felt as though God Himself had wrapped His arms around me and assured me of His protection and provision for the rest of my life. I thought immediately of a psalm of David:

The LORD is my light and my salvation;
Whom shall I fear?
The LORD is the strength of my life;
Of whom shall I be afraid? (Ps. 27:1)

I did not accept that this sense of God's protection would wear off in a few weeks, and I would be left bereft and despairing. I committed myself afresh to the Holy One of Israel who would indeed be my *Jehovah-jireh* for the remainder of my days. I was eager to learn what God had in store for me in this new life.

One outcome of Tony's death was a sympathy card and letter from Irene, in which she showed genuine sadness at my loss. She had always greatly respected Tony. I thought a great deal about this absurd seventeen-year breach of ours and decided it was as good a time as any to write to Irene and ask to visit them again. This time she wrote back, welcoming me to come whenever convenient.

I returned to Florida that autumn, and soon after opening up the house and getting settled into my life there, I drove up to Ohio to present myself at her door. It was somewhat unnerving, as I wondered how they would take me and how our conversations would go. But again I was reminded: "Whom shall I fear? . . . Of whom shall I be afraid?"

I was warmly welcomed into their home. Don had recently retired from the ministry, and they had moved to Cambridge, a small town in southern Ohio. It was clear from the first that there would be no frank discussion of the lapse since 1984. It was just "pretend as usual," which was obviously how she preferred it. But we were able to discuss Tony at length, his work in recent years, and his sudden illness. I was touched by their concern and love for Tony.

One person was not discussed—my daughter, Sue. Irene asked about Jon and Chris and their families and that was all. Nevertheless, I left Cambridge feeling it had been a successful visit and had no doubt that future ones might be even more fruitful.

I took the opportunity to drive over into Pennsylvania before returning south, and the person I most wanted to see was

"Momma Ruth" Schwenk. It was a delight to be in that dear old house once more and share precious days with Ruth. We were able to discuss everything together, the family problems and disappointments as well as the blessings. Ruth reminded me, "But Vicki, *everything* that happens to you is from God's hand! Irene's attitude included! God has given you exactly the family He wishes you to have, for your growth, faith, and His glory!"

I had recently reread a book that had caused quite a stir in the 1970s called *From Prison to Praise*. The author, an army chaplain, advised people who came to him with a multitude of crises to "praise the Lord" for them, whether they were marriage problems, financial difficulties, or health issues. He tried to show them that as we give thanks for all things, we increase our faith in God and He in turn can bless us "more than we ask or think." Some refused to see the sense in giving God praise for the troubles in their lives or, even more, for those who had sinned against them.

But I was beginning to see that my reservations about Irene were working against God's plans for me. He wanted me to depend on Him for everything and not doubt. And I was finally beginning to see that God had put Irene and me into our family for His own purposes. Who was I to complain about this?

Praising God for adversity does not come naturally to any of us. But that can be no excuse for living in the flesh, when Jesus sent the Holy Spirit to dwell within us and to provide us with supernatural help in this world. Clearly this meant that one could have this help in a bad marriage or with difficult children or coworkers or bosses who were making life a misery. Then, and especially then, it was time to praise the Lord!

Again Ruth was reinforcing the scriptural secret of holy living—nothing happens to the child of God but that He allows it for our benefit and His glory!

I completed that extraordinary journey with fresh convictions that I didn't intend to waste further time complaining about family members or friends or neighbors, because *God* had arranged my life in such a way as to allow me to grow into the person He had in mind all along. Why do we make things so hard for ourselves?

My English summer of 2001 was almost gone and I was enjoying doing school runs to pick up four-year-old Thomas, Chris's son, in the reception class at the Altrincham Preparatory School nearby. It was a wonderful school that Chris and Jon had both attended. The staff strives to get the most out of the pupils from the age of four. Tom often bounded out the door with other blonde-haired little boys, almost identical in their short gray pants and maroon blazers, gray shirts and gray and maroon striped ties. Sometimes I had to squint to make sure the one I beckoned over to the car was actually my grandson! He always enjoyed ducking behind this one or that, and hiding from me just to tease. He was the apple of my eye.

Then it was September, and in another month or two I'd be preparing to return to the USA. I was getting more attached to Thomas and hated to think of leaving him for six months. "Don't you dare grow a minute older!" I'd plead, and he would laugh.

That afternoon I parked the car next to the school gates and turned on the radio to await his arrival. It was 3:00 p.m. (10:00 a.m. in New York) and suddenly I heard the unimaginable news—the New York Trade Center was hit by two planes, and the towers were falling. I thought of the thousands that worked within, and the deplorable loss of life. *Dear Lord, what is happening?* I couldn't stop weeping.

The next thing I knew Thomas was knocking on the window, asking to be let in. He looked at my face and asked, "What's wrong, Mom-Mom?"

I said, "Oh Thomas, some very wicked men just killed an awful lot of people . . ."

Then he asked me, "Does Jesus love the wicked men as much as the good men?"

❦ CHAPTER THIRTY-ONE

In the days to come we learned all the hideous details of the terrorists, some of whom did their air training in a flying school only a few miles from my Florida home. We could scarcely comprehend such evil. It seemed to commence an even more dark and violent period in our world's history.

And we were now obliged to expect more stringent traveling regulations than ever before—new rules and restrictions, being frisked like criminals, even having to take off one's shoes and show the underside of our feet. Preparations to board now took hours rather than minutes. Something told us we were going to have to get used to these new and painful routines.

I decided to bypass the complications of air travel for once and drive to California that next spring. I planned a trip traveling on I-10 almost all the way, detouring once or twice to hit Route 66. It was a return in time to the innocent days before terrorists tried to take over the world. Thanks to the computer, I found bed and breakfasts in a convenient line clear across the country, and I took seven days to drive from Florida to California. It was a wonderful experience, staying in a few grand southern mansions, a doll's house of a cottage in Texas, a charming adobe house in New Mexico and an old hotel on Route 66 in Arizona hung with pictures of cowboys lounging against the front of the hotel in 1900.

I'd rise around five in the morning and be on the road soon afterward, often before the sun peeked over the horizon. I usually drove around five hundred miles a day and arrived at my destinations in the early afternoon. And although the trip was a fantastic experience, I was glad to cross the border into California and arrive at Sue's Pasadena home a few hours later.

I spent several relaxing weeks with Sue, visiting our favorite spots along the coast and restaurants we loved. I traveled between Sue's Pasadena house and the Santa Barbara home of my beloved aunt and uncle, Rita and Will Harley. In those years I felt so blessed being able to visit with them regularly too.

Finally I was on the road once more, having to retrace my steps almost three thousand miles back to Florida. I took a slightly more northern route, getting to explore a few new areas of the country, and all went well until I hit Oklahoma. I arrived at a beautiful antebellum southern mansion late one sunny afternoon. I awoke the next morning to a fierce snow and sleet storm. I didn't give it a thought until I was on the road and large trucks kept passing me and splashing up icy snow onto my windshield, making it nearly impossible to see the road before me.

I should have stopped and turned around. But I didn't, and twelve hours later my weary bones limped into my next destination in Memphis, Tennessee. It was still raining, but at least the temperature had risen. It was dark now, and I was lost. I drove into a gas station, stopped the car, threw open the door and tumbled out. Disoriented, I gashed my head on the sharp door corner and watched as the blood rushed down my face into a rain puddle at my feet. I felt dizzy and didn't know what to do.

I stood there leaning against the car for a few moments. Suddenly a black youth appeared and asked, "May I help you?"

With the door still wide open, I gratefully accepted his arm as he led me into the gas station and sat me down. Then I remembered I'd left my keys, phone, and purse on the car seat, and asked him to kindly get them for me. He rushed off and returned with my possessions. He led me to the ladies' room where a black woman was exiting. She took one look at me and my bloody face and said, "I'm a nurse just come off my shift. Let me bandage that for you!" The young man accepted my grateful thanks and disappeared. The nurse quickly gathered some items from the store and dressed my deep wound.

I reported this horrifying incident to my sons when I was safely home. They were aghast that I would naively allow a stranger to collect my keys, phone, and purse to bring to me, when he could have easily grabbed all and disappeared. "Don't you see?" I told them. "The Lord is my keeper! I will not fear what man can do to me!" It was another incident that proved His unfailing love and protection. I was convinced that He allowed that accident to show me once again that as my Husband, He would keep me safe. That rainy night in Memphis remains a blessed memory. "He shall give His angels charge over you, to keep you in all your ways" (Ps. 91:11).

Irene and I had resumed our correspondence, and she asked me to visit them again on my return. I knew that Irene had been struggling with kidney failure for the past few years, and her life became dependent on dialysis three times a week. She often had to return to the hospital when a treatment failed.

I drove up to Ohio once more before returning to England,

and I noticed this time how thin she was, with bruised arms from the many injections she suffered. I asked to accompany her as she went for her dialysis treatment, but I was unprepared for the chilling sight of ten patients all sitting rigidly still in their large armchairs, with wires and equipment protruding to and from the machinery all around them. It was like coming into a sci-fi horror film. Irene explained that it was imperative that each patient remain perfectly still for the sessions, which took three or more hours. I could not begin to imagine what a terrible ordeal it was for her, three times a week. And when there was a problem with a vein, the nurses would have to grope around her upper and lower arms or even her neck, to find a suitable port.

After an agonizingly long afternoon at the treatment center, Irene was released from the equipment, and another session was over. I had a new appreciation for her condition and the painful process that kept her alive. I thought that if I were in her position, I would decline further treatment.

I thought of Tony's response to hearing about his inoperable cancer and his decision not to prolong his life with chemotherapy. It was exactly my mother's reaction, too, when she was told about her cancer. Both of them chose rather to accept the prognosis with calm and faith rather than to add further suffering to their pain-wracked bodies. I vowed that I would chose that way too, when my time came.

After we returned to their home, Irene relaxed quietly and was grateful for a few days of rest before the next treatment, but the time immediately following a session left her very weak. Even so, we talked quietly and enjoyed each other's company. To my surprise, Irene asked me to tell her about my Sue. And then, "Why don't you bring her to visit me on your next trip?"

CHAPTER THIRTY-TWO

I couldn't wait to get back to Florida and phone Sue to report what Irene had suggested. Would she be willing to fly out to see her? Sue had always felt very protective of me when I related our lifelong conflicts, culminating in our seventeen-year estrangement after Sue came back into my life.

Nevertheless, I had learned that Sue didn't hold grudges and was often generous to those who had wronged or slighted her. She was willing to give people the benefit of the doubt. It was yet another thing I loved about my daughter. And she didn't hesitate to accept Irene's invitation. We began planning the big reunion which would take place the following year.

Meanwhile, I was preparing for a special houseguest from England who would stay with me for two weeks and speak at various churches and house groups during his visit. My friend was Laurence Levine, a Messianic Jew who had founded his own messianic assembly in Northumberland. Over twenty-five years earlier I had been asked by my friend Pam to have my hair done at the salon in neighboring Sale, where Laurence was a stylist. Pam explained that she had found a new hairdresser, with whom she had shared her faith in Jesus Christ, and that he seemed to listen intently. She suggested to me that evening, "Why don't you go to the salon, and you can tell him about your life in Jesus too?"

So the following week I was greeted by a twenty-seven-year-old Jewish man with an Afro hairstyle, a large Mexican mustache, flowered shirt, bell-bottom trousers, and platform shoes—the perfect fashion of the day in the 1970s. He was soft-spoken and very courteous, and he asked many questions that reflected a genuine interest. In the days that followed, Pam invited him to a Bible study in her home, and to our surprise and joy, he attended.

Laurence had long been searching for something more in life and had dabbled for a time in Transcendental Meditation, Mormonism, and the growing drug culture. But as he continued to attend the Bible studies, he realized that here was truth that he had not faced before. In fact, having studied at a Hebrew school from his earliest years, he had a good knowledge of the Old Testament. Now he was finding the completion of his studies as he faced the claims of Jesus as the Messiah long anticipated by his people.

One night as we sat around Pam's living room, a current chorus was sung, and it was the moment when Laurence came home to Yeshua—"for the Jew first and also for the Greek" (Rom. 1:16). He raced from the room, rushed upstairs, and felt the presence of the Holy Spirit entering him and making sense of life at long last.

Within a few short weeks, Laurence became transformed before our eyes. The big Afro disappeared and a softer style—including a trim beard and mustache—took its place. His flower-power clothes were exchanged for modest shirts and jeans. He took on the appearance of Jesus to us, especially as he held out his arms and began to pray in the meetings.

That year Laurence realized that God had something other than hairdressing in his future. He took a Bible course and quickly showed us that he had a real gift for ministry. That New

Year's Eve we had a wonderful celebration service in which he and a Palestinian Christian friend, Mike, put their arms around each other and gave thanks and praise to their Lord—a moment we will never forget.

Over a quarter of a century later, Laurence was still traveling up and down England, Scotland, and Wales, sharing the gospel of Yeshua the Messiah, bringing the teaching of Passover to churches, and helping Christians better understand their Jewish roots. I thought it would be great to introduce him to my Florida Christian family and some of the church fellowships nearby. I wrote and asked him, "If I send you a ticket, would you come?"

He replied, "Is the Chief Rabbi Jewish?"

I met Laurence at the Orlando airport and the next few weeks were a blessed experience for those who heard him minister and proved to be a blessing to Laurence himself. For me, I could only marvel at the transforming power of Jesus Christ to save those who seem such unlikely candidates for His church. When people scoff and say, "People never change," I not only think of myself, a prodigal daughter who has been overwhelmed with the love and mercy of God, but I always remember Laurence, a hippy hairdresser who gave up all to follow his Messiah.

That following summer in England, I decided to join a two-week ocean-going cruise to St. Petersburg, Russia. It was designed as a Baltic cruise, taking in the capitals of each of the Scandinavian countries, Poland, Germany, and finally Russia. Tony and I had taken a more modest Danube cruise many years earlier, on a canal boat rather than a seventy-six-thousand-ton ship carrying two-thousand passengers. I was encouraged by other cruising enthusiasts to go, even though I was planning to travel alone and pay the premium for a single cabin. Everyone would be so friendly, they insisted, and I was ready for the adventure. What I longed for above all was to visit the churches of Russia, and I hoped, to attend a service or two and hear the wonderful music I'd heard so much about.

It was indeed a unique experience, although my memories of the exotic cities of Stockholm, Copenhagen, Helsinki, and Oslo tended to blend together on my return home. I managed to enter beautiful churches in Poland and Germany as well, but sadly our two days in Russia had no opportunities for church services. The hours were taken up with visits to palaces, the exquisite Hermitage Museum, a gargantuan banquet at the magnificent Astoria Hotel, and a joyous evening of folk music and dancing at a nearby concert theater. I managed to stand outside the closed Church of Our Saviour's Blood and try to imagine what a service there might be like. Perhaps my imagination of it exceeded the reality.

Sue and I eagerly planned our next special event—a visit to Irene and Don in Ohio. It was a meeting we never expected to happen. I planned to once again drive up from Florida and meet Sue at Columbus airport. We had booked a week's stay at a log cabin in an apple orchard just outside of Zanesville, which would give us many hours on our own, but with plenty of time to be with my sister as well. I was confident that the Lord was drawing us together for His purposes, and I prayed that there would be a loving and open atmosphere between the four of us at all times.

The apple-orchard cabin was a wonderful surprise, and we sat out on the porch watching deer roam among the trees. There was a floor to ceiling stone fireplace with logs to burn at night, and we each had our own room and bath. It was a perfect choice for a restful time on our own.

This was my third visit to Irene in recent years, and as she opened the door, I saw that she had grown thinner still, paler, and more stooped. But she greeted me warmly, and then hugged Sue so enthusiastically that my daughter looked somewhat shocked. Irene couldn't get her eyes off Sue. It caught me by surprise too.

Irene asked all about Sue's studies and career, and I was amused to take a backseat as she peppered her with questions. We went to a favorite restaurant that night, and Sue was again the center of attention with the conversation continuing around her life, interests, and talents. I realized that Irene was enormously impressed with Sue, and it surprised and pleased me.

I was happy to see that Irene had somehow come to life during our visit, despite her declining health and constant treatment. I could not have expected a more successful visit. And just before we left, Irene took Sue's hands in hers and pleaded, "Please won't you come again? Just come on your own any time!"

As I drove Sue back to Columbus for her flight home, we agreed that we didn't know what to make of Irene's pressing invitation to Sue. All those years that she refused to recognize her! What could have caused such a change?

I had a partial answer in one of Irene's next letters. She said she always wondered why I was unwilling to give Sue to her. I suspected that Irene had resented me for preventing her from raising my daughter.

I tried to explain in my next letter that I had never expected either my parents or sister to learn about my pregnancy. I went to the Salvation Army to keep it a secret and felt that giving the child up for adoption was the only way of solving my problem. Thus my agreement to give her to the Josephs was a *fait accompli*—I couldn't undo it even if I were to change my mind. But the thought of a mother giving her child to her sister to raise would be an intolerable burden! To see one's child being raised by another, with no say or input in her upbringing! I was appalled to think of it.

But it explained yet another cause for Irene's resentment and bitterness—she felt she should have been given the chance to raise my flesh and blood.

CHAPTER THIRTY-THREE

I returned to England for the summer, to the emerald green grass and leaves, and May blossoms on the trees. I was always surprised anew to see the rich foliage and colors of Cheshire parks and gardens.

It has been, after all, my adopted home for almost five decades, and when I think of England, it is *home*, despite the fact that Chris and Jon had long since gone to other parts of the world to work and live. Tony's sister, Margaret, had recently passed away, so there were few relatives left to me there. Nevertheless, I cherished some great friends that were true sisters or brothers to me. Most of all, I believed that God had planned for me to live the bulk of my life in England, where He intended to use me as a witness of His love and mercy to all who call upon Him.

Soon after my return, I was visited by my great friend Sister Philomena, a Loreto nun for sixty years. Philo had been Mother Superior at three British convents and was, in her eighties, still active at the Welsh convent where she now lived. She was called out regularly to take this or that elderly nun to the hospital or for medical appointments. Sometimes when we tried to get together for a brief trip, we were thwarted by Philo's work at the convent. But we did manage some great road trips or outings across the

Welsh mountains during the summer months. It was good to see her so soon after my return home.

I first met Sister Philo when she was headmistress at a Loreto school in Manchester. She was a tough no-nonsense Irishwoman who surely put the fear of God into her students. But we warmed to each other—an Irish Catholic and an American Mennonite. That was decades earlier, and now we were closer than ever.

I often wondered what my mother would say about my friendship with Philo! In those days, Mennonites didn't establish ties with Catholics, and I recall my mother warning me that "the worst Mennonite was better than the best Catholic." It was made clear that we should not associate with "those people."

I was glad that such prejudices didn't hold any longer. My mother changed her rigid opinions in later years, as did many other Mennonites. Nevertheless, it was a unique experience for me to welcome Philo and other Loreto sisters into my home for our Bible studies back in the 1980s. As they sat there, in their black and white habits, I couldn't help thinking, *What would mother say!*

But the habits changed too, and now the sisters wore navy skirts and sweaters, and colored blouses, and there wasn't a head covering to be seen. I often enjoyed visiting Philo in the convent in Llandudno and always shared Holy Communion with the sisters. They seemed quite happy to have this Protestant partaking of the Eucharist with them. We may have silently disagreed on some aspects of our faith, but the centrality of Christ our Redeemer and Lord was undisputed.

I was watching a BBC documentary on Wells Cathedral when I got a sudden urge to see it for myself. It was about a five-hour drive down to Somerset but I thought it would be an enriching experience to spend a few days there. I should have known by now that a "sudden urge" is often a message from my loving heavenly Father.

I booked a room through the Internet in a sixteenth-century farmhouse about a mile from the cathedral. I planned to stay a few nights. The farmhouse didn't disappoint—it was a beautiful old building, carefully but not overly restored. Up the creaky staircase to deposit my case and then I was off to inspect the cathedral.

What a spectacular sight! It dwarfed all the surrounding cottages, homes, and hotels. It was a divine statement: *You can build your little houses, but I will reside over all and point the way heavenward!* I thought surely a man would be blind indeed to fail to recognize the majesty of God in that place!

I sat in the back of the vast sanctuary and worshiped the Lord. I was overwhelmed with thanksgiving for His goodness and grace to me, even in this small way, bringing me to this magnificent place. As I silently praised Him, I observed a small commotion near the high altar. There were seats being arranged, a cluster of people in discussion, and away to the left, a young man in jeans and T-shirt went over to the piano and looked down on it. Probably a piano tuner, I thought.

Then to my amazement, he sat down and began to play like an angel from heaven. Not just any song, but my all-time favorite: Rachmaninoff's Second Piano Concerto! That was the CD that haunted me so in 1984. I kept playing it over and over in the months before Sue phoned me that July. It was a shock to me when she told me she was listening to that very recording when Betty rang her to say I had written, asking about her. It changed everything for us!

I sat there and the tears flowed as that ordinary-looking young man played like Rachmaninoff himself. Finally musicians appeared carrying their instruments. As they sat down and began to tune up, a conductor came forward, and they all began at the beginning. An usher informed me that the orchestra was rehearsing for a special concert that night. The young pianist was a famous Russian who had won many awards. And there was I, with a handful of worshipers, treated to a free concert that would cost £30 a seat in a few hours!

That afternoon was a surprise in another way. After the rehearsal was finished, I took out a small notebook and began to write in it—about my life, my Lord, and how He had led me thus far. It turned out that the entire visit to Wells was one touch of God after another.

One of my Bowdon neighbors is a remarkable woman named Kath Blears. Kath and her husband, Mike, are Anglicans who live around the corner from Beech Lawn. They are a retired couple in their 70s who travel between their home in Bowdon and a holiday home in the south of Spain. Some years earlier they had prayed for a new ministry, and when they visited a missionary couple in Kenya, they both felt that God had a job for them there with the children of Kenya. They began to search for a suitable plot of land so that they might build an orphanage or school on it. They had no intention of soliciting funds for this venture; they were prepared to put their own savings to the Lord's use.

When they first made their plans known to a nearby Kenyan Baptist bishop, he eagerly invited them to use some of his church property, free of charge, on which to build an orphanage. They welcomed his offer and invested $30,000 of their savings into the design and building. Mike carefully chose the workmen and oversaw the development. When the building was completed, they planned to hire personnel and ask local authorities to provide the neediest children for their home.

Suddenly the bishop let them know that he would choose the staff and decide which children would come. It was clear to Kath and Mike that he planned to move in on the venture and take over the project. It was a shock to the Blears to realize they had been deceived by a Christian minister. After much prayer they decided to walk away from their investment and start afresh. Although it was a disappointment, it taught them that they needed to trust God alone and insist on total honesty amongst everyone that shared their vision.

They were advised by a trusted official that what was most needed in that area was a school for the many village children that could not afford a private education. Mike and Kath immediately planned to build a school and to open it for the first three grades and expand each year.

After the building was complete, the retired couple flew to Kenya and set out in the excessive heat and humidity, walking from village to village. They hung posters on trees, inviting villagers to bring their children to the new school where they would be given a free education, Christian instruction, uniforms, school supplies, and books. It must have seemed too good to be true for the many illiterate families who did not imagine their children might someday learn to read and write.

Kath happened to mention the school to me during a morning visit, and I plied her with questions about the project. She had photographs of the growing school, of the sixty village children in the first three classes that were fed, clothed, and instructed at the school free of charge. She and Mike had hired an administrator, cook, three teachers, a groundsman and other part-time workers as needed. The couple flew to Kenya several times a year to oversee new building projects as the school grew and more pupils were added. They continued to carefully administer their own funds to get maximum benefit for the children.

I was eager to sponsor one of the children, and I was given a photo of a handsome laughing little boy named Wilson. I fell in love with him immediately. I wrote him letters, but although he was learning Swahili and English in school, as a five-year-old he was not yet proficient enough to read my letters, so his teacher obliged. I have photographs of her stooping down to the little boy, reading my messages, with his laughing face asking, "Read it again!"

Wilson was raised in a nominal Muslim family by a single mother who also had two younger sons. They were very poor and lived in a small shack with a dirt floor, no windows, and no furniture. The mother had to work in another village, selling what few wares she could afford to buy. She was grateful that Wilson could attend the school, even though he had to walk several miles each way on hot dusty roads and through other inhospitable areas. Wilson became a leader even at that young age, and his enthusiasm was a challenge to other pupils older than himself. He loved singing the school theme song, "I Have Decided to Follow Jesus," each morning and led the school at the front of the line, marching in time to the music.

I was devastated when Kath returned from a trip to Kenya and reported that Wilson had died of a savage attack by rabid dogs. The pupils and teachers alike were heartbroken. He was so very greatly loved and not yet six years old.

I wrote a small book, *An Angel Named Wilson*, which we published with photographs of our dear boy and the schoolchildren of Michael James School. It was translated into Swahili and English, and each child received a copy to take home to read to their illiterate parents. The people were amazed that their own children, as young as six or seven, were able to read a book to them!

I was scheduled for an operation that summer, and as much as I dreaded it and would have preferred to refuse it, friends and family pressed me to have the procedure. There had been tests the previous year, just before I left for Florida, and the results had shown cancerous cells. A hysterectomy was recommended. But I had always said that if I should have cancer like my mother and husband, I would decline treatment. I thought of friends who had suffered many long years from cancer and although they prolonged their lives by enduring chemotherapy, they eventually succumbed to that disease. I believed that my mother and husband had been wise to decline treatment. But my family was insistent, and so I agreed to have the operation which I was assured was "routine."

Before setting off for the hospital that July, I invited my friend Owen Lowery and his new wife to have tea with me at Beech Lawn. We always managed to see each other during my summers in England, either at his home nearby or at my own. He had weathered years of treatment in hospitals, and often when I had to cope with something particularly disagreeable, I'd think of Owen and his remarkable courage in the face of unimaginable disability.

I had written Owen's story years earlier, shortly after his accident on a judo mat that left him a quadriplegic and unable to breathe on his own. He was just eighteen at the time, holding numerous British medals or trophies as the best in his weight class. He was in training for the Olympics when he suffered the injury.

I had read about him in the Sunday Times and felt the urge to meet him. He was still in the hospital then, flat on his back, but he was happy to answer my questions and talk about himself. His mother, Sybil, sat by his side, remarkably cheerful for a woman who would have to devote herself to his care for years to come. He experienced a Christian conversion through the witness of two judo players who came to share their faith with him. That prompted me to write an article about him for a Christian journal, which ultimately developed into a book.

Observers might have assumed life was just about finished for Owen. But thanks to the new advances in computers, he was able to order the latest computer including a device that looked like earphones with a straw attachment. He could blow into the straw and thus "type" on the computer screen. He became so proficient with this that he could "type" as quickly as anyone seeking out the keys with their fingers.

Owen had loved sports most of all during his school days, but that didn't mean he wasn't a bright student if the subject interested him. When he was well enough to leave the hospital and return to his newly adapted home, he was able to sit up at the computer screen, and read or write about whatever appealed to him.

In recent years he had received a bachelor's degree and graduated with honors. Then he took an interest in military history and earned a master's degree again with honors. It was about this time that he began writing poetry, and once he started, he never stopped. He completed the course work for his PhD, with the theme of the World War I poets, but he has also published several books of poetry which have impressed the critics.

Owen's emails are always beautifully written, witty, and charming. He is upbeat and interested in everything. He would not take kindly to being pitied. But he is a unique inspiration. I planned to take my thoughts of Owen with me to the hospital.

CHAPTER THIRTY-FOUR

I was told I would be kept in the hospital for four or five days, but after the operation, I became very ill with infections, and by the second week, I was sure I would not survive. Truly, I didn't even want to. I wasn't told what was happening, but I was too weak to eat or even sip water. I felt that I was struggling to climb a mountain, and I knew I would not make it. All the plans I'd made for the future didn't seem so important now. I just wanted the Lord to take me home!

One day during the third week, Kath Blears came for another visit. I told her I was losing the fight, and she looked at me so lovingly and said, "Oh, Vicki, you must give it all to Jesus . . ."—for a split second I resented that—". . . as I had to do," she continued, "when Michael ended his own life."

Those words suddenly brought me back to where I needed to be. Kath's faith when her beloved son committed suicide was an inspiration to so many. She and Mike had not known the depth of Michael's depression until it was too late. But she threw herself on Jesus alone and was enveloped with His peace.

It was after that tragedy that Kath and Mike planned to do something in Michael's memory, and the Michael James School was born.

I will never forget Kath's loving reminder for me to put my

weakness and despair on the Lord Jesus. It snapped me out of my self-pity in seconds!

I was released from the hospital after four weeks, but the infections had taken their toll and further complications meant there would be another operation necessary in the months to come.

During my convalescence I received an email from Sue that she planned to fly to Pennsylvania to visit her aging Joseph relatives and wanted to finally get acquainted with Ruth Schwenk who lived in the general area. I wondered what she would think of Ruth and what Ruth would think of her!

I wondered whether Sue would be eager to share with Ruth her love of astrology and the way she was convinced that the heavens revealed themselves in peoples' lives. Dear Sue was so enthusiastic that she never waited for an invitation to let people know the things that mattered most to her. I loved that about her, but I also wondered whether Ruth was the right person to hear all about Sue's love of astrology. And what would Ruth advise her to do?

Sue spent two days with Ruth at her home in Cressona, feeling comfortable enough to tell her all about her earlier life and what her interests were now. During their time together she took Ruth to her favorite mountaintop restaurant for a memorable meal. When Sue returned to California, she was anxious to tell me how much she loved Ruth and what a wonderful, positive person she was, so attentive to everything Sue had to say. "Ruth was everything—and more—that you described!" Sue exclaimed.

I asked, "What did she say when you told her about your plans to write a book on astrology?"

"Oh, she just smiled and nodded in that lovely way of hers," Sue chuckled. "She seemed very interested."

It answered my question about what Ruth would think. Would she gently lecture Sue about the subject, or would she just smile and leave it all to the Lord to sort out? I was not surprised at Ruth's reaction. I might have known!

I was able to combine my next visit to Irene in Ohio with a brief side trip to see Ruth again. My visit to Pennsylvania coincided with Mother's Day and I looked forward to having a special celebration with Momma Ruth at that time.

I had booked a meal in her special restaurant, but that afternoon I suggested we first stop at the local garden center and pick up a plant or two of Ruth's choice. It was a beautiful day and when Ruth came down the stairs. I was amazed at how handsome she looked, almost six feet tall, in a white wool blazer over a white crocheted top, and white wool trousers. A fine looking woman for ninety-two!

Together we walked up and down the crowded aisles of plants and flowers, and then I walked ahead up a ramp. As I turned to look back, I saw Ruth stumble on a loose mat, and simultaneously a large metal rack of pots slowly tipped over and a sharp corner of the rack struck Ruth's forehead. I watched in horror as this dear tall woman slowly fell sideways. With blood already flowing, she landed flat out on the stone floor. Her face was dripping with blood, and her white jacket, top, and trousers were all splattered red. I cried out as I looked at my precious friend. And that wounded face looked as calm as if she were sitting in her favorite rocking chair with a cup of tea.

"I'm fine," she smiled, looking up at me, almost amused.

Of course there were employees and visitors scrambling around, looking for a chair for her to sit on. Strong arms lifted her up and helped her to the chair while a clerk rushed off to call for an ambulance. She kept smiling, insisting that everything was all right, and thanked everyone profusely for their kindness.

The paramedics arrived swiftly and wanted to put her on a stretcher and take her to the hospital. "Oh, that's not necessary," Ruth laughed. "I'll be perfectly okay when Vicki takes me home."

The men opened a wheelchair and took her to my car and helped her in. "You see," she told them, "my Lord Jesus looks after me, and I have nothing to worry about."

They looked at poor Ruth's clothing, all splattered with blood, and her face and hair as well. They tried to encourage her to get checked out at the hospital, but she was just as persistent that there was no point.

When we returned home, I helped her get changed, and she settled back into her rocking chair. I was still upset with what had happened, but Ruth chuckled and told me it was all in God's plan. "I do believe He allowed that for your sake," she said finally.

"Why for my sake?" I was puzzled.

"It was just another object lesson to show you how nothing happens to the child of God that is not for her good and His glory."

At the time I hated to think that frightful incident was for my sake. But since then that vivid picture has stayed with me to show how God sometimes allows us to sacrifice ourselves to teach or bless others. It reminded me of the words I read at Tony's funeral that summarized his life: "So then death is working in us, but life in you" (2 Cor. 4:12).

❧ CHAPTER THIRTY-FIVE

I returned to the USA in November and within a few weeks resumed my monthly visits to a very special friend, Tommy Zeigler, who has been living on death row for the past thirty-nine years. It has been one of the worst cases of injustice I have ever known. Years earlier a journalist friend happened to mention that she'd interviewed a man on death row twenty-five years earlier and that he was still there. She told me a book had been written about him and numerous websites discussed his case, all of which cited the disturbing details of his trial—evidence that had been withheld by the State, perjured testimony by a detective, and a biased judge.

I thought at first, yes, most people on death row say they're not guilty. But I ordered the book anyway and read it with increasing disbelief that such a miscarriage of justice was still being played out. Tommy, of Winter Garden, Florida, was a devout Baptist and well-known businessman who was shot and critically injured Christmas Eve 1975, in his furniture store. He was unaware that before he arrived, his wife, Eunice, and her parents had stopped to pick up a Christmas gift. They and another man were shot dead, lying in another area of the very large store.

Within minutes of arriving at the scene, a young rookie detective decided that Tommy killed the four and shot himself, although six guns were found on the premises and all had been wiped clean. It was the start of a nightmare that has yet to end. After a quick trial, the judge overruled the jury's recommendation and sentenced Tommy to death. He has been living in virtual solitary confinement in a six-foot by eight-foot cell since 1976. He continues to have a strong faith in the Lord, trusting that someday he will be vindicated.

My journalist friend and others also retained their hope and prayers and support of Tommy, convinced that he was wrongly charged and convicted. I learned that there have been hundreds of death row inmates throughout the USA who were freed thanks to DNA testing, with Florida and Texas leading the way with the most reversed convictions.

But inexplicably, Tommy's DNA tests did not free him. He had claimed all along that he never touched his father-in-law—he never knew he was in the store—but at his trial the State made the case that he held his father-in-law in a headlock and beat him to death. The prosecutor "proved" this by displaying the bloody shirt Tommy wore that night. Tommy had always said that the blood was that of a black customer, Charlie Mays, with whom he had grappled before he was shot. The DNA tests proved that the blood on his shirt was indeed Mays's blood, and his father-in-law's clothing had not a trace of Tommy's blood. Mays's DNA was found on the father-in-law's shirt.

Tommy had asked for DNA tests in 1987, when he first learned of the new testing that might free him. Years went by before the State was willing to grant this, but even so, the test results did not appear until 2002. And then the State said, "Well, it doesn't matter. Tommy is guilty anyway." Tommy's lawyers tried to get more DNA testing, but these requests were continually denied. Most appeals, when new evidence is discovered, are repeatedly denied as "procedurally barred" or "time barred."

These are rules invented by the very system that should want above all else to seek the truth.

When I first learned of Tommy's situation, I was told he welcomed correspondence. I was glad to add my letters of support and assurance of prayers to the others. I couldn't imagine how he could survive all those years and retain his sanity. But God was giving him strength to live a life that would destroy anyone who didn't know the Lord.

Several years ago, I began monthly visits to him during my "Florida season." It was a sobering experience to sit with him in the death row café. It was also sobering to see other men there, some young, some old, having visits with wives or family or friends. Many of them didn't look any different from one's friends or neighbors. Some were there because of just one mad moment of wickedness. And perhaps some, like Tommy, shouldn't have been there at all.

I had flown to Florida in uncertain health, knowing that I had at least two operations to deal with on my return home. But I was determined to celebrate my eightieth birthday by flying to California and staying with my daughter, Sue, in Pasadena. She spared no effort as usual to give me a fabulous visit. And I also made sure of spending time visiting my dear cousins Jan and Jim Brown in Santa Barbara.

Sue kindly arranged for me to see a specialist at UCLA Medical Center, who confirmed that I was likely to need another operation, the result of careless work at my local hospital. I was sorry to admit to my American family and friends that I had been badly let down by Britain's National Health Service (NHS), when for forty-seven previous years in England my family and I had experienced only the very best of care. I had always been an enthusiastic supporter of the NHS since arriving in England in 1966. But on this one occasion, I was very disappointed.

Nevertheless, I was learning that God does not allow anything to happen to His child that is not for his good and God's glory. "All things work together for good to those who love God, to those who are the called according to His purpose" (Rom. 8:28). I had happily memorized that verse as a child in Sunday school. But in recent years I was faced with the sobering urgency of *living* it.

Sue and I were excited about our plans to travel to Pennsylvania and this time spend a few days with Momma Ruth together. She was now ninety-three years old and had fallen again since the garden center accident. I hated to think of that dear woman in pain, but knowing Ruth so well, I supposed she wouldn't have minded.

Just three days before we were to meet her, we received news that she had fallen once more, was in a coma, and was not expected to live. A day later we learned that our beloved Ruth was in God's presence. She had been an important presence in my life since I was a child, but now it was time for me to live in Christ without depending on Ruth to advise or encourage me. "Only Jesus" must be my goal.

At about the same time, Irene was entering her tenth year of dialysis treatment, and she longed to be able to stop it. I spoke to her on the phone and advised her to discontinue treatment. I be-

lieved it was a painless way to go and that the patient would simply drift into a coma. I tried to assure her that the Lord would
look after her and also look after the family she left behind. But
it was not a painless slipping away as we'd hoped, and her family
was distressed to see her in great anguish in her final hours.

I regret deeply that we never did have that frank conversation that would have been good for both of us. I have over the
years come to accept that God gave me Irene for my own development. I also believe that He gave me to Irene, to enrich her
faith. But I'm not sure that she ever really accepted this.

CHAPTER THIRTY-SIX

To my great surprise, I received a letter from Irene's husband, Don, soon after her death. In it he said he wished to fly to Florida to see me. I was dumbfounded, recalling the decades of disapproval I felt from both of them. Was he now, perhaps, wanting to explain why both he and Irene had distanced themselves from me for so long? I felt that now he might be willing to give me the answers I waited for all those years.

I replied that of course he could come. I drove to Orlando to pick him up and was surprised at how old and vulnerable he looked. He had always been such a formidable figure, not only in the pulpit, but whenever we met.

During the next few days, he spoke of nothing but Irene. Tears flowed as he described how much he missed her and how devastated he was by her death. It surprised me that one who seemed so sure of his faith and counseled others during bereavement was now powerless to put into practice what he had preached for decades. I tried to share with him some of the Scriptures that had meant so much to me after Tony's death. But it seemed that nothing comforted him.

Before he left, I hoped I might have some answers about Irene and how she felt about me in the months before she died.

The final night I asked him, "Tell me, Don, do you feel that Irene ever forgave me?"

He looked up from his book and thought for a minute. "Well, of course," he replied and went back to his reading. He made no further comment.

When Don returned to Ohio, he wrote and thanked me for the visit, which he claimed was very helpful. As for me, I was as much in the dark as before.

In recent years, Irene's daughter and I have carried on an email correspondence which has helped us both try to better understand the mystery that was my sister. When Susan had finally managed to contact her birth mother, she wrote to me about the reunion, and how much she was looking forward to developing the relationship.

Then in May 2000, the occasion of Susan's fortieth birthday, her husband, Brad, wanted to treat her to a special birthday party. His parents planned to fly in from California, and other family members would attend the special event held on a paddle steamer leaving from the waterfront in Cincinnati. Susan and Brad wanted to invite Hedy and Wolf too and introduce them to the family, but she feared Irene's anger and for a long time the couple didn't know what to do.

Finally Susan decided it would be unfair not to invite her birth mother for her very first family occasion. She was disappointed when Hedy and her husband declined, pleading another engagement. But at least she was then free to invite her parents and tell them of the great plans Brad made.

"I will not come if *that woman* is coming!" Irene reminded her hotly. Susan was able to assure her that no, Hedy would not appear. It was, Susan felt, perhaps the best thing, as it would avoid any unpleasantness to mar the day.

The party promised to be a magnificent and memorable affair, with special music and a banquet held on the well-decorated boat. All anticipated a happy occasion with so many family members in attendance. But soon after the guests were seated, Susan became aware of Irene's angry voice raised as she spoke to Brad's parents, complaining about Susan's "betrayal." She had her back to Susan and Brad but Susan could see her in-law's dilemma as they were obliged to listen to Irene's angry comments and were unable to escape them. For the whole of the afternoon, Irene sat with her back to Susan, refusing to speak with her. Susan fought back her tears, but at the end of the evening she wept. "I'm so sorry I invited her!"

That started the estrangement between them that lasted for almost ten years. I felt Susan and I had so much in common!

In the spring of 2013, I was happy to welcome at long last Susan and Brad into my Florida home. From the moment of their arrival, I felt such love for that dear couple that they seemed like my own children. Susan was able to fill me in about her early life, and the years she struggled to feel her mother's love and approval. My heart went out to her. *How could anyone not cherish this beautiful daughter?* We had such happy days together that I hated to see them leave. I told Susan that I admired her for her gentle Christian witness and refusal to get discouraged or bitter. She told me, "You have given me more love and affirmation in this one weekend than I have felt in all my life." I could have wept.

As they stood at the door, I couldn't resist teasing, "Please, may I adopt you two?" They invited me to spend a week with them in Ohio before returning to England.

I flew up the week before Easter. It was an idyllic time, getting further acquainted, meeting their children and their mates. I attended their large church where Susan is a counselor, and we had delightful visits to neighboring towns with old-time shops, cinemas, and restaurants. And of course we had long talks about her growing up years—how she always felt pressured to make the best appearances and impressions in church, school, and neighborhood, but never felt that unconditional mother's love that she longed for.

While I had for years supposed that it was Irene's stern preacher husband that caused her to hold me at arm's length, Susan disagreed. She assured me that Irene was the one who made all the emotional decisions and that Don just followed her lead. Susan described how Irene's anguish about being barren colored her social and church life, preventing her from enjoying other women's infants, and thus she became increasingly isolated from friends. Don tried his best to help her, but the bitterness was so deep-rooted, she could not let go of it.

"I always felt she had almost an obsession with all the photographs she took of you as children," I said. Irene collected a multitude of photos long before the advent of iPhones and iPads, and stacks of photo albums filled a full wall of shelves around the fireplace in their home. She seemed to have a passion for freezing every event with countless portrayals of her "perfect" children, smiling, perfectly dressed, and perfectly presented as a family living a perfect life. So it was sad to learn from Susan that the smiles did not accurately convey the tensions that made up much of the family life.

I visited Don several afternoons in his assisted living apartment nearby, and Susan and I drove over there for a final visit before I returned to Florida. Although sometimes confused and frustrated, he was in good spirits that afternoon, so I felt encouraged to ask him, "Tell me something, Don. Why did Irene call your daughter *Sue* when she knew the Josephs had named my child *Sue*?"

He thought for a moment and said, "Well, she always liked the name Sue."

Susan and I laughed as I said, "Oh come on, Don. You can do better than that!"

Later that day, Susan told me of a chat she'd had with her father a month or so earlier. She was pressing him to recall whether he and Irene ever had a frank conversation about her great disappointment and resentment.

Don said, "I asked her many times why she could not just give that issue to the Lord, and once I even told her that her pride was keeping her from having peace about it. But she got very angry at that and wouldn't discuss it. The next day she came and apologized, and she admitted that I was right."

Don said he then asked Irene, "Would you like me to write to Vicki to come up again, and talk with you about it?"

"No, it would be too embarrassing," she said, shutting the door on further comment.

On my final evening, Susan and Brad's family came together for a meal and conversation, and we talked about adoption from Susan's viewpoint as well as my own. Susan spoke of her years trying to develop a deeper relationship with her birth mother, which was often one-sided, as Hedy was regularly depressed and in poor health. I described the blessing of my relationship with my daughter, Sue, and how we loved and respected each other. It didn't always work out that way with some, I said. Often the newly discovered birth mother is unwilling to incorporate the lost child into her life, or the child cannot throw off the bitterness of feeling abandoned years earlier.

I knew that God had given me an extraordinary second chance with my Sue, and I believed also that now He was unexpectedly giving me this new relationship with Irene's daughter. I was feeling doubly blessed!

Finally Susan's son Tyler asked me, "What would you say is one of the most important lessons you've learned in your life that you could pass on to us?" I didn't have to think long. I said I believed that God gives us the family members He wants for us—both the loving ones and the troublesome ones, and sometimes especially the troublesome ones—as they are all meant to help us grow stronger in Him and become the people He planned for us to be.

A month later, after returning to England, I wrote to Susan on her birthday:

To my dearest "adopted daughter"—my other Sue:
I am so blessed to have found you and Brad at this late stage in my life, and so grateful that God has given us to each other. It's sad that it has taken us all these years to really know one another. But I'm just tickled pink that we're a great extended family now! I think you are the best, both of you, and I applaud you for the wonderful way you have raised your children to love the Lord. I'm

so proud of them too! I pray we'll celebrate many more birthdays together.

All my love, Aunt Vicki

I was overjoyed at Susan's reply, in which she called me "Mom"! Who could have imagined that God was planning to give me yet another Susan to cherish? How mysterious yet wonderful are His ways!

In the 1970s, our home was often open to guest speakers and evangelists who came from the USA to travel and speak in England and surrounding countries. One such evangelist was a dynamic Messianic Jew who prophesied over our family during his visit with us. In the prophecy he quoted a verse in Isaiah 54: "All thy children shall be taught of the LORD, and great shall be the peace of thy children" (v. 13 KJV).

This startled me, because I immediately thought of my secret child, known only to a few. "All thy children" denotes more than two, and I willingly accepted that word from the Lord that my daughter, living somewhere in the USA, would be taught of the Lord as well as my sons. That was the first message I had received about her since the days in the hospital when I was holding her in my arms.

I was subsequently thankful that Sue had indeed been taught of the Lord and had a clear knowledge of God's Word and God's leading. I continued to believe that all three of my children would experience the great peace that I was enjoying, in devoting life and future to our wonderful God and Savior.

Then, on other occasions, I was impressed with a verse from another favorite chapter, Isaiah 43:

I will bring your descendants from the east,
And gather you from the west;
I will say to the north, "Give them up!"
And to the south, "Do not keep them back!"
Bring My sons from afar,
And my daughters from the ends of the earth (vv. 5–6).

I seemed to keep running into this remarkable prophetic word. I realized it pertained first of all to Israel and then to the church, foretelling all the strands that come together in the blessing of God to those who trust in Him. But one commentator singles out verse six as a "strand of adoption," and I dared to take that to my heart. Over the years I have felt Him lovingly giving me other children whom I love and call my godsons and goddaughters. Each of them has been as much a gift to me as I may have been to them—folk from many different countries who have crossed my path in the plan of God and "enlarged my tent." But these were not sons and daughters I had chosen for myself; they were God's gifts!

There were and are beloved sisters and brothers, too, like my "big sister" Jean Brobst, Irene's best friend from Mennonite days, whose backyard adjoined the Josephs' all those years ago, and who "just happened" to mention to my sister about the adopted baby girl that had arrived at the Joseph home in July 1955. For many years Jean has been a precious sister to me, and only the other day I received another letter from her:

Dear Vera (I like that much better),

Thanks so much for your newsy letter. Sorry it's so inconvenient having to send a letter, not an email, to this old lady who still lives in the dark ages. I'm not about to change, so you're stuck with it.

I'm so glad to hear about you and Susan in Ohio becoming so close. May the Lord bless you both!

My health is good, but my osteoporosis and arthritis keep me on a walker. But I can stay in my own home and have a good number of friends who minister to me.

My family is well and mostly healthy. One great joy is my grandson and wife who are missionaries in Guatemala. It's been a miracle in many ways.

I'm so sorry to hear about your health problems. But as you said, it is all for our good.

Please tell Sue in California to call me with details of your surgery and your prognosis. I really want to keep up with your progress so I can pray intelligently. The Lord richly bless you in the days ahead. I'll be praying for you!

With love, your big sister, Jean

❧ CHAPTER THIRTY-SEVEN

E aster Sunday, 2014. I saw a church sign in the morning as I was driving to a nearby Easter service:

Remember the One Who Created the Bunny

I am a passionate supporter of the Church of England when I'm home in Britain, but often my churchgoing in the USA takes me back to the religious culture of my childhood. My memories of Mennonite services are never far from my mind. I can vividly recall the moment seventy-five years ago when I walked to the altar at Bethel Church to "accept Jesus into my heart" and my father's prayers as I knelt by his side. I recall equally vividly the outdoor pavilion services at Mizpah Grove, the nightly meetings with choirs singing the old-fashioned hymns, and the congregation fanning themselves with cardboard fans advertising the local funeral parlors. I remember old Sammy Guile sitting in a front row, waving his handkerchief in the air and praising the Lord. He seemed ancient at the time. He was probably younger than I am now. But his face is still before me.

I was raised in a Mennonite culture, and although I accepted this as natural as a child, in my teen years I rebelled as few if any other Mennonite girls of my age even thought of doing. I look back and marvel that God never gave up on me—indeed, He protected and directed me in spite of myself.

When I attend a local Nazarene church in Florida, I enter a twenty-first-century version of the Mennonite culture. We sing the same grand old songs, and the format of the services is not unlike the Mennonite ones. When I recently attended their Easter service, I was transported back to the Easter services I knew as a child. Sunrise services were held at an Allentown cemetery, and we huddled together in a group on those chilly mornings against the cold wall of the mausoleum where bodies were buried in a crypt. We'd sing "Up from the Grave He Arose." I can never sing that song without thinking of the grave stones in the darkened lawns around us and that icy mausoleum with walls of marble drawers holding the remains of the dead.

I still retain a deep love of my Mennonite roots. I am forever grateful to God for the wonderful teaching instilled in me as a child. I consider myself so blessed to have been given that heritage.

But I have learned that although many if not all denominations were started as a result of real zeal for God, many denominations today are a sad specter of what they once were. Man moves in on a beautiful work of God and crudely paints his own amateurish picture over the masterpiece God wrought. People bicker and fight about dogmas and doctrines. Many pastors take their talents and success too seriously and lust after more acceptance and acclaim.

In this twenty-first century, churches advertise with slogans and catchphrases or devise trendy new church names that could refer to a dance hall or beer garden. I passed a neon sign the other day that read, *UPLIFT! An exciting new service!* and I wondered where Jesus Christ fit into this picture. When I drive from my Florida home to relatives in Jacksonville, I pass a large modern church which advertises one Christian celebrity preacher after another on a billboard—*Come and hear the great A (or B or C) on Sunday at 7:30!*—as if they are more worthy to be listened to than Jesus Christ Himself. It is a sad modern custom, this promoting of our worship of the Lord God like a television show. We hawk services to the public as if selling automobiles, and Jesus Christ is often conspicuously absent.

Recently there was an article in Britain's *Daily Telegraph* which reported that within two decades, there may be more active Christians in China than in the USA. That's hard to believe when one observes the churches on nearly every street corner in US towns and cities—many newly constructed, with huge parking lots filled to capacity on days like Easter Sunday.

But the health of the American church may not be as robust as we think. Fabulous new buildings and elaborate church programs are not an accurate gauge of the true health of the invisible church of Jesus Christ. In China, the political climate there actually helps the people avoid the pitfalls of building programs and outward appearances. The true church was and is their personal devotion and dedication to Jesus Christ and His gospel and their willingness to sacrifice everything for Him.

We Americans are great at building theme parks and casinos that promise much but are essentially business empires. Those who live abroad sometimes think the American church culture is not unlike these models. Our Christian culture may be in danger of producing a political or cultural "churchianity" rather than a true family of Christ-followers. Jesus' warning to the Pharisees, that they were "whitewashed tombs" (Matt. 23:27), is a warning to the American church to make sure that personally and corporately, we are scrubbed clean inside and not merely a flashy outward show.

Recently I set out to visit my friend Tommy Zeigler on death row again, my final visit before flying back to England for the summer. Tommy has not attended a church service in thirty-eight years. He once wrote to me that he rises between five and six in the morning, exercises in his confined space, and then reads his Bible and worships alone. And I suspect that his faith is far stronger than multitudes of American Christians who attend services once or more each week.

I drove my car up Route 301 to Starke and turned at the sign pointing left to the *State Prison*. It always sends shivers through me. The road runs through a gentle quiet suburban area of older ranch homes and a few churches, then opens out onto the flat, barren prison property. Just ahead are the high wire fences and somber gray buildings. Death row is just one of these, called the P Dorm.

There are personal details to present, inspection, inventory, metal detectors, five locked gates and a long caged path to travel before finally arriving at the death row café. In it, for the only time in their prison lives, prisoners are able to sit at bolted-down chairs and tables across from friends or relatives and share snacks, burgers, or colas, and pretend they are normal human beings having an indoor picnic.

I am always amazed to note how cheerful Tommy is when he comes through the inmate's door. He and other inmates greet each other with the camaraderie of members of a football team. This time he related the most recent setback in his lawyers' attempt to revisit an appeal that the state had rejected. He knows the appeal process is a cruel joke on inmates that merely gets their hopes up in an otherwise intolerable existence. He knows that 99.9 percent of appeals are denied. But still he and the others pin all their dreams on a reversal. It is all they have.

But this time he admitted to me that he would rather die than carry on. He was ready for God to take him, and his thoughts were now on meeting the Lord and being united at long last with his beloved Eunice. I touched his arm and could only grieve with him in silence.

CHAPTER THIRTY-EIGHT

When Tony and I moved from our large house, Copperfield, in the 1980s to an apartment at nearby Beech Lawn, two of our first guests were Peggy and Ken Johnson, of Virginia Beach, Virginia, two very old friends from Grace Chapel days. Peggy had cross-stitched for me a lovely plaque which almost forty years later still hangs in my kitchen:

> Everywhere is home to me,
> for Christ is everywhere
> and He is my home.

I think of my late dear friend Peggy when I look at that text, because she surely lived those words. The Johnsons were a military family that lived in twenty-five houses in as many years, from bases in Japan and Hawaii to Europe and all over the USA. They were at home everywhere because their Lord Jesus was first in their lives and was with them wherever they went.

But I also think of it as my own mission statement: *The Lord Jesus Christ is my home.* St. Mary's Bowdon may be my earthly spiritual home, but Christ Himself is my home, now and in the life to come.

When we read of the great saints of the church, in the early church, in the Middle Ages, and in recent centuries, we find they all have one discovery in common. Whatever their background or persuasion, they had single-mindedly discovered Christ as their home, the one constant in their lives, though they were living in a changeable and dangerous world. He was called by the prophet Isaiah "Wonderful, Counselor, Mighty God, Everlasting Father, Prince of Peace" (Isa. 9:6). John the Baptist saw Him approach and called out, "Behold! The Lamb of God who takes away the sin of the world!" (John 1:29). And Jesus, the Word made flesh, had to explain to His disciples who asked to see the Father, "Have I been with you so long, and yet you have not known Me . . . ? He who has seen Me has seen the Father" (John 14:9).

Those of the past and present who have had a life-changing encounter with Jesus Christ put church buildings and agendas, doctrines and dogmas further down the list of priorities. Nothing in life is of greater importance than an encounter with the One who told the Pharisees "Before Abraham was, I AM" (John 8:58). And that encounter *must* lead to a life of constant abiding in Him. It is the only life worth living!

The other day I learned about a Christian minister in Iran called Farshid Fathi. Prior to his arrest in December 2010, he was a respected church leader. He has now been in Evin prison, Tehran, for over three years. After enduring 361 days of solitary confinement, he shared the mystery of God's presence in suffering:

> My wilderness is painful, but lovely.
> Some parts of my wilderness are covered with thorns
>   and hurt my feet, but I love it, and that's why I call
>   it "lovely pain."
> My wilderness is like an endless road, but short
>   compared to eternity.

My wilderness is dry, but an oasis with the Holy
    Spirit's rain.
My wilderness seems to be a lonely trip, but I am not
    alone.
My Beloved is with me: not only Him, but my faithful
    brothers and sisters; I carry them all in my heart.
My wilderness is dangerous, but safe . . . because I dwell
    between His shoulders.
So I love my wilderness, because it takes me to the
    deeper part of You, Lord,
and no one can separate me from Your arms forever.

Farshid was sentenced to six years imprisonment. We just learned that he had his foot broken by a guard stamping on his bare foot as he went to help another prisoner. It was three days before they took him to a hospital.

This account of a modern martyr reminds me of Richard Wumbrandt, who served fourteen years in Romanian prisons until the late 1960s. In the 1970s I attended a meeting at a nearby Methodist church where he was speaking. I didn't know anything about him but when he walked to the pulpit I was aware of a glow about him and the most beautiful, serene face. I thought instantly, *Now there's a man who has never suffered!* I didn't know how wrong I was.

His first words were, "My name is Peace . . . because my Father's name is Peace. My name is Love . . . because my Father's name is Love." He went on to instruct us that we adopt the name of our earthly father in life, but, he asked, what characteristics do we live and carry with us? Is it the name of our *heavenly* Father: Peace? Joy? Love? He began sharing about all those years when he was imprisoned and tortured for his faith. But that's when the attributes of his Father were reflected in him. He told of two years of solitary confinement, and the alienation from family and friends. But at no other time was he more aware of the presence of God and the joy he experienced as a result.

I thought, too, of Watchman Nee, imprisoned in China for twenty years for his faith. During that time he was forbidden to write even the name of God to his wife in his letters. But in one he wrote simply, "I maintain my joy." It told her everything!

Dietrich Bonhoeffer, age thirty-eight, bid farewell to his fellow prisoners in April 1945 and walked to his execution with calm and even joy that blessed and encouraged them all. His words still profoundly affect us today.

These are men who lived the writings of St. Paul: "For to me to live is Christ" (Phil. 1:21). They could not have survived without knowing Him intimately.

Mahatma Gandhi once remarked, "If every Christian in India lived as Jesus Christ, there wouldn't be a Hindu left in our country." This could also be said of the USA or Britain, as nominal Christianity must give way to uncompromising Spirit-filled Christ-followers if we are to "turn the world upside down" again (see Acts 17:6).

CHAPTER THIRTY-NINE

My maternal grandmother, Viola Grace Barclay Harley, was a gifted poet. When my sister and I were very young, Grandmother Harley wrote a beautiful poem which my father set to music and taught to us. Over the years we sang it many times in various churches and on Allentown's WSAN Sunday-night radio programs. Although I learned the words at an early age and sang them many times, they have never meant as much to me as in recent years.

> I think He's wonderful, don't you,
> To lay aside His majesty,
> And condescend to come and shed
> His precious blood for you and me?
> What matchless grace, that He should bear
> The penalty that was our due,
> This undefiled, pure, sinless One!
> I think He's wonderful, don't you?
>
> I think He's wonderful, don't you,
> To intercede for you and me.
> Our great High Priest with tireless zeal

Defends our blood-bought victory?
And when the enemy condemns,
Five bleeding wounds He bears anew,
'Til every accusation's stilled.
I think He's wonderful, don't you?

I think He's wonderful, don't you,
To make a home for you and me,
Where we may in His presence dwell
From taint of sin, forever free?
Dear Savior, Intercessor, Lord,
May we Thy wondrous person view,
And every ransomed soul shall cry,
"I think He's wonderful, don't you?"

My grandmother didn't have an easy life, but you could not have found a more cheerful, contented woman, when well into her 70s she was still writing poetry, editing manuscripts, and also working as a secretary in our Mennonite church. I recall the many times she entertained the family with her recitations, either of her own poetry or those of others. I cannot ever recall her with anything but a smile on that dear face.

In her later years, she was quite deaf, and then her eyesight started to fade. But she never stopped smiling. In the spring of 1955 she wrote her final poem, "Thy Healing Touch":

Lord, keep me close, I care not how
For I know Thou wilt not allow
One trial too many, one grief too much;
For though to earthly sounds my ears are dead,
With Thy sweet promises my soul is fed,
Until, please God, there comes Thy healing touch!

Lord, keep me close, I care not how . . . I find myself repeating these words over and over these days, as the uncertainty of life is reinforced by the hospital letters dropping through my mailbox. I am no longer in control of my weeks and months. I am required on a specific date to appear for this test or that examination. Then finally the letter comes which tells me the date of my first operation. All my plans are shelved as health issues take priority.

But the National Health Service is not in control of me. I am more aware than ever before that God Himself is in control and that nothing will happen to me that is not part of His great plan. The text constantly in my mind and heart during the days after Tony's death is as appropriate now as it was then: "The LORD is the strength of my life; Of whom shall I be afraid?" (Ps. 27:1). That doesn't mean I don't pray for Him to bless the hands of the surgeon or the care I receive after the operation. But unlike some Christians, I do not feel I should command this or that from my God, who knows the circumstances and consequences infinitely better than I do. It is enough for me that He has promised to "not leave me nor forsake me" (Ps. 27:9) and that He has assured me of His peace—"not as the world gives do I give unto you" (John 14:27). It is enough for me!

Recently I've been enjoying reading a book by Paul Tournier, with the title, *Learn to Grow Old*. He writes about the need for accepting the changes that come our way, and the way acceptance can ease the transition between middle age and old age. Acceptance also helps us prepare for death.

But as I read I was reminded of the need to accept many limitations we all face in life, whether physical, mental, or emotional ones. At the same time my friend Owen was learning to adjust to the physical limitations placed on him through his fall, a British policeman was shot and paralyzed as he tried to foil a robbery. Owen started at once to prepare for a totally new life in which he was obliged to accept great changes. The policeman refused to accept such limitations and later took his own life. These were both strong men who exerted mental and physical strength in their chosen lives. But in the one case, Owen was willing to consider that God would help him through this devastating period. The policeman rejected many kindly Christian approaches and refused to consider a life of disability.

But even many Christians find it hard or even impossible to accept trials or disappointments when their lives turn out to be very different from the ones they would choose. "I'd never forgive God if He took my son!" said one mother. It's such a tragedy that even my dear sister, raised by godly parents to trust God in all things, could not accept her "thorn in the flesh."

Then I think of the many dedicated single missionary women like Amy Carmichael, who accepted God's plans rather than their own. I think of her when I read that verse in Isaiah 54, "For the [spiritual] children of the desolate one will be more than the children of the married wife, says the Lord" (v. 1 AB). Only the Lord knows how many of these women have been blessed a thousandfold with countless spiritual children.

And again I marvel at how Tommy Zeigler has gone on, year after year, the victim of grave injustice, but constantly trusting that God will bring something good out of his trials. He knows, of course, that he has nothing to fear. "If they execute me," he told me recently, "I know where I'm going." Meanwhile, he accepts that God has His reasons for allowing him to spend almost forty years on death row. "Maybe it will help to expose and defeat the evils of the death penalty," he told me during our last visit together.

CHAPTER FORTY

*L*ord, *keep me close . . . I care not how . . .* That phrase was sliding across my mind for days, before I realized its fuller significance. I was aware of a series of frustrations, one after the other, a worrying pattern that I began to suspect would get worse.

A friend said, "Oh, the devil must be mad at you!" But I couldn't accept this. I was certain that God was in control of my life. He wouldn't step aside and permit old Screwtape to terrorize one of His little ones. I was no Job.

As if to confirm this, I read this prayer in a book by Isobel Kuhn: *Lord, if this trial is from You, I accept it. If not, I command the devil to go in Jesus' name.*

The week I was certain I was being tested started with two car bumps in one day. A woman backed into my car and the bumper crunched. I hastily backed up to avoid more damage and crashed into a pole, landing in a gulley. Damage front and rear in the space of a minute. The woman climbed out, smiling. "I guess it was 50-50, wasn't it?"

Well, *no.* But I didn't want my insurance to rise, so we agreed to leave it.

The next day I fell prey to a debit card scam and I lost £300. The day after that, I got two parking tickets in one afternoon for incorrectly placing my disability badge wrong side up.

I prayed, *Lord, if this is from you . . . !*

I confess, I get impatient with frustrations, with bureaucracy. Mad, even. It was only a few days later that my bank's computer was torturing me by refusing to accept my change of address despite repeated phone calls and three visits into the branch to attempt to sort it out. And their brazen slogan is "Helpful Banking!"

Over the next few weeks there were confrontations with call centers connected to British Telecom, the gas company and the Trafford Council. Then my computer needed fixing. I would happily dispense with the accursed phone, but I need the computer desperately. Hours, even days, were wasted with these frustrations.

Wasted? *Lord, keep me close . . .* I was indeed seeing a pattern. But this was no sudden phenomenon. I'd been thinking a good deal about last summer's operation that went badly wrong. The four days' hospital stay that turned into four weeks. The terrible and needless infections that caused further damage requiring repairs this summer. I tried not to grumble outwardly, but I did not accept this well. I recall many silent mutterings about the nurses who wouldn't come when called or who would come, say "just a minute . . ." and then disappear for an hour or more. On reflection I was being tested last summer, and that one I failed. So perhaps the Lord was making me repeat the examination this year.

I recalled when I was in the depth of despair and dear friend Kath lovingly admonished me to "give it all to Jesus." Yes, I did that and confessed my self-pity, but it wasn't too long before the grumbles about poor hospital care surfaced once again.

I am often impatient, critical, and intolerant of unreasonable regulations and red tape. One might say this is justified. But when we claim to live in the Spirit, are we entitled to exercise fleshly tantrums? WWJD, indeed!

This morning's test caught me unprepared. A friend sent me an email with a pretty bad grammatical error. I teasingly pointed it out in my reply. I was shocked at her answer: *You are far from perfect, you know.*

It was like a punch in the stomach. I had meant no harm! In fact I was pointing out something to help her in her work. I couldn't stop thinking of the injustice of it! I fretted and paced for an hour, wondering how I could respond to this unkind comment. But what was wrong with me? I was overreacting to something that was *absolutely true.* I had to laugh. I knew full well I was far from perfect!

I looked down at a small book of Bible quotations on my desk. There were some pages of quotations about humility. As I began to read them, I was astonished at how quickly the flesh goes on the defensive, even—or especially—when an accusation is true. I thought how easily one who claims to love the Lord Jesus Christ can fail a simple test from a loving Father. I stopped to thank Him right then for exposing a problem that needed to be dealt with. I have often quoted the verse "I have been crucified with Christ; it is no longer I who live, but Christ lives in me" (Gal. 2:20). It shocked me to see how easy it is to claim a position in Christ and yet not live it. That's another lesson that will have to be learned over and over.

As the date for my next surgery approached, I could not shake off the feeling that this could be my biggest test yet. Well-meaning friends often assured me, "Oh, you'll be fine," but I was also aware of the surgeon's warnings about possible side effects. Before last year's operation, I paid no attention to similar warnings and was unprepared for the infections and loss of abdominal muscle that followed, requiring more surgery this year. I grumbled over the treatment and mistakes that were made, and I listened to those who sympathized and urged me to sue. I wrote the strongest letter to the hospital administrator, and my self-justification grew with each passing day. His reply angered me—the hospital was not to blame, and the surgeon did all according to the book. It was "just one of those things."

I was alternatively in prayer for God's answers and indignant that my condition was worsening. But I couldn't deny the Scriptures that kept returning to my mind and spirit that I had read at Tony's funeral.

> Always carrying about in the body the dying of the Lord Jesus, that the life of Jesus also may be manifested in our body. For we who live are always delivered to death for Jesus' sake, that the life of Jesus also may be manifested in our mortal flesh. So then death is working in us, but life in you. (2 Cor. 4:10–12)

As if to emphasize the point, I came across Madame Guyon's autobiography once more. I had read it years ago, and suddenly there she was again, offering her testimony of dying to self that the life of the Lord Jesus would be manifest to others. All during the nights leading up to the operation, I read and reflected on her message of taking up her cross for Jesus' sake. I recalled reading it years earlier and thinking she sometimes seemed to look for trouble and abuse! This time I did not think that. I knew she was being led on the Calvary road to bring Jesus' life to others, and now God was again appealing for me to travel that road.

The Calvary road . . . it reminded me of a little book by that name, authored by Roy Hession, that I had read decades earlier. He encouraged me to accept a deeper walk with Christ. His words were daring me to take steps of greater abandon than I had taken.

Tony and I had been living in New Jersey in the early years of

our marriage when we learned that Roy Hession was sch
to speak at a church in New York. We decided to go and li
him. As with the book, his sermon was a strong appeal to commit one's all to Jesus, regardless of the consequences. We were
both affected by his message, although it would be years before
either of us dared to take that step of greater faith.

At the close of the service, the resident pastor got up and
thanked Rev. Hession for coming, adding, "But we cannot agree
with his message, as it does not conform to the beliefs of the
founder of our denomination." He proceeded to dismiss all that
had been so earnestly preached. I watched Roy Hession as he sat
on the platform with his head bowed. I grieved for him, for his
humiliation, and the way his heart's cry was so trampled upon. I
thought about that night a great deal and was saddened that he
had been so cruelly rejected.

All these years later, I thought of him once again and realized
I was mistaken in feeling sorry for him. I saw that Roy Hession
was not only preaching the way of the cross, he was living it. He
knew that just as surely as Christ was rejected and humiliated, we
who follow Him should not be surprised to expect similar treatment. When such things take place, we are truly "carrying about
in the body the dying of the Lord Jesus." There's no room for
self-justification or self-preservation. Our enemy is not the person who condemns or criticizes us; our enemy is the self-life that
prefers a comfortable existence as opposed to the Calvary road.

And to make certain that I got the message this time, God
put another book in my hands by Basilea Schlink with medita-
tions on the passion of Jesus—the same message of the sacrificial life that brings fruit and life to others. It reminded me of
all the books, all the signposts along the way that titillated my
mind with stories of bravery and sacrifice, but did not produce
a similar step of obedience to put *all* on the altar! If there is a

danger in the many published stories of heroism and sacrifice of the saints of old, it is that readers can mistake the reading and enjoyment of the stories as a substitute for living the life.

A little chorus keeps coming into my head these days, learned and sung frequently at baptismal services so long ago. As crowds of Mennonites stood around at the old Jordan River in Allentown, and the pastor led new Christians into the waters of baptism, we would sing:

Where He leads me, I will follow,
Where He leads me, I will follow,
I'll go with Him, with Him all the way!

from "Where He Leads Me" by Ernest W. Blandy (1890)

Now, over seventy years later, I sing that with new determination—*wherever He leads me.*

CHAPTER FORTY-ONE

The taxi dropped me off at Salford Royal on the morning of my next operation. It was like arriving at an airport terminal, with massive modern buildings in various colors, and the yawning mouth of a revolving door wide enough to accommodate a variety of conveyances. Inside, a cheerful lounging area with sofas, tables, and chairs led to a concourse filled with shops, a restaurant, even a mini supermarket, a clothing kiosk, a chemist, and a book and magazine store. The spacious lobby belied the grim work going on in the bowels of the institution.

There were forms to fill out (ah, the NHS meets the twenty-first century!) and people to ask me the same questions over and over. Finally I was wheeled into the room adjoining the "theatre" (the Brits have such elegant language for the most utilitarian places) and averted my eyes as the needle was slipped into my hand.

"Vera! Vera, wake up. Wake up now; open your eyes . . ." Someone was choking me, holding me down. No, it was a restraint of some sort around my neck. Oh, the bandages, so tight I found it difficult to breathe. And the mask over my mouth didn't help. I wanted to push it all away, but I could not move. I had woken to a nightmare of hell.

I was told I was being prepared for Intensive Care. Intensive Care? Why? They would say only that the operation took longer than expected—over six hours—and that it was now early evening. I was whisked away, before I had the chance (or strength) to ask further questions. I was rushed through brightly lit corridors into a sci-fi world of computers, monitors, and other equipment beeping and blinking away. White-robed assistants each sat at the foot of a given bed, not to look at the patient lying there helplessly but to stare at the variety of screens and charts and figures thereon. I learned quickly enough that I was just a slab of flesh, that the *real* me was the list of vital signs and lines going up or down on the screens. All eyes were fixed, day and night, to those screens. There was no time, or inclination, to address the pain-filled patient lying there helplessly.

It began an agonizing night and day of torture, with hours crawling like a tortoise. I felt shut off from every human contact. At a time when one most needs, even desperately craves, the human touch, there was no room for such indulgence. The equipment was everything!

They had swiftly turned me here and there, slapping disks to a dozen or more parts of my body attached to wires attached to yet another monitor. I had a drain running from the wound in my neck and another drain further south. There was a tube feeding me. It was a great relief when after some hours my face mask was removed and a tiny tube supplied me with oxygen through my nose. But as for the rest of me, I felt as if I were being crucified—held down, unable to move, abandoned. The sluggishness as I fought off the anesthetic was as bad as the pain in my neck, but worse still was the feeling of claustrophobia, a panic that I had never experienced before.

All night long I was kept awake with the sounds of machinery beeping away, the hushed voices of staff laughing and whispering to each other but not to me. I thought of Tommy, trapped in that isolated six-foot by eight-foot cell for thirty-eight years. What was a night or two or even a week of this, compared to his imprisonment? Still, that gave me no release from the feeling of panic and desperation.

It takes grace and patience to be a good patient

Eventually I was able to slip out of that despair and concentrate on why I was there. On one level, it was a growth that doctors advised me to deal with two years earlier. I had put it off, not wanting to think about it. On a deeper level, God was using this experience to teach me patience; He knew how badly I needed it!

As dawn came, a nurse actually presented herself at my bedside with a cup of tea—my first human contact in an eternity. How desperately humans need a touch from other living beings! *Man cannot exist by machinery alone*, I thought.

Late that afternoon I was relieved to learn that I was being sent to a ward for normal recuperation. The bits and wires were removed from my person, oxygen was deemed unnecessary, and I was beginning to feel human again. I began to scold myself for being such a ninny for panicking about something that lasted for less than twenty-four hours.

I reentered the land of normal illnesses and felt grateful. If the nurses here were only marginally more attentive, we patients could at least communicate freely with each other—a huge boon to recovery. I began to count my blessings.

I was ushered to my bed just inside the door and immediately a nurse pointed to the whiteboard above my bed. Before even asking me my name, she said "What matters most to you?" I looked at her in amazement. "You know," she tried to explain, "family?

Getting home? Recovering?" I laughed and said, "The Lord, of course!" She looked puzzled and then wrote it down. And so my testimony was listed there above my bed for all to see. I loved it!

In the days that followed I was able to meditate more clearly on the sacrifice of Jesus Christ for mankind. I recalled years ago asking teenagers in Sunday school if they could remember the first lamb that was sacrificed for sins in the Bible. Only once did I get the right answer—when God had to provide proper clothing for Adam and Eve! Their own attempts to cover themselves were inadequate, I reminded them, just as our man-made efforts are inadequate to provide a cloak to cover our sins. Then I shared with them the passage in Genesis where we read of God's great plan in His message to Abraham: "God will provide Himself the lamb for a burnt offering" (Gen. 22:8).

I fear that too often in our churches, the message of Christ's sacrifice is not preached clearly enough. I've often thought that the difference between Anglican and Baptist clergy is that the Baptist assumes everyone is a sinner, while the Anglican assumes everyone is a Christian. I worry when clergymen assume we know—or believe—more than we do. If even a regular churchgoer can have difficulty explaining the basics of faith, what hope is there for the ordinary man on the street? Some time ago I heard of a young woman working in a jewelry store who was asked by a customer to show her some crosses. "Well," she said, "we have these plain ones, or you can have one with a little man on it." How can we be sure ordinary folk understand why "a little man" was hanging on the cross?

I thought again of the thread of redemption through sacrifice that runs like a scarlet cord throughout the Old Testament and into the New, showing God's promise to "provide Himself the lamb" to cleanse us from our sins. Modern man often scoffs at such a religion, and yet he understands Jesus' words, "Greater love has no one than this, than to lay down one's life for his friends"

(John 15:13). It is a familiar enough phrase used to bear tribu soldiers who die in battle. But it is more properly used to descrive Jesus Himself, who stood before Pilate and said, "For this cause I have come into the world, that I should bear witness to the truth" (John 18:37). He was the Lamb of God, who would die for all those who trusted in Him as their Savior and Lord. He was and is the "Lamb," who even now stretches forth His hands to a sick and violent world, willing to heal and forgive all who come to Him. When we are offered the privilege of taking the bread and the wine to remember His sacrifice, we are continually opening up ourselves to receive His life and His Death into our beings.

Having been set aside for even a few days was refreshment to my soul, but I was looking forward to attending the hospital Communion service that Sunday morning. I was amazed that those nice ladies who lived monotonous days in bed or in a bedside chair would not want to attend an inspiring service that was available to them. Ah, well. The porter arrived on time and whisked me away down long corridors and into a charming little chapel with a chaplain waiting for us. There were just six of us lined up in wheelchairs ready to join in the beautiful service of hymns and Communion.

When I survey the wondrous cross,
On which the Prince of glory died,
My richest gain I count but loss,
And pour contempt on all my pride.

Were the whole realm of nature mine,
That were a present far too small,
Love so amazing, so divine,
Demands my soul, my life, my all.

from "When I Survey the Wondrous Cross" by Issac Watts (1707)

Later that day my faithful friend Rhona arrived to take me home. Once more I thanked God for His deliverance and protection, and the healing that had surprised us all. I was humbled to learn just how many people in the US and UK were praying for me. Even Tommy Zeigler and his death row prayer group had been praying for me!

That same week the American TV channel Investigative Discovery (ID) presented a documentary by the French Canadian producer Christian Bruyère about Tommy, entitled, "A Question of Innocence." Friends who watched it were outraged at such injustice. I would have to wait to see it for myself until my return to the US later in the year. The important question was this: would the politicians dare to watch it? What would they do about it? I had written several letters to President Obama in past years about Tommy but never received a reply. Politicians don't like to second-guess even a verdict as bad as that one. Would anyone dare to stand up for him after all these years? Only the Lord knew.

CHAPTER FORTY-TWO

It had been thirty years since that extraordinary day in July 1984 when I first heard a sweet unfamiliar voice say, "Mrs. Holland? This is Susan Joseph" and almost thirty years to the month since we finally came face-to-face in that Allentown driveway. We agreed that 2014 would be a good time to celebrate our thirtieth anniversary—and so Sue flew in from California to arrive at Manchester Airport in September for a very special reunion.

I arranged a busy schedule for her during the two weeks of her stay, which included visits to Cambridge, Stratford-upon-Avon, and Wales. But I was especially anxious for her to meet friends and neighbors, my church family, and others who had learned something of that secret daughter who had so unexpectedly reappeared into my life three decades earlier.

The first item on our agenda, however, was a return to Salford Royal Hospital to meet with the surgeon who wished to discuss my recent CT scan and help me decide on the appropriate treatment. Sue and I felt it right to proceed with the abdominal operation despite risks, and Mr. Lees put me down for a date in November. I was aware that this was the most complex operation of my life, but I knew I was in God's hands.

Immediately after leaving the hospital, we drove southeast to Cambridge where we had booked a room for a weekend conference Sue wanted to attend. Her recent articles had been accepted for publication by the British Astrological Association and she hoped to meet the editor and other colleagues there. She planned to attend the Saturday seminars while I explored the city of Cambridge for the first time in my forty-eight years of living in the UK.

I was particularly eager to tour King's College chapel recalling memorable Christmas TV programs of "Lessons and Carols from King's." Crowds of tourists from every country thronged the sidewalks, and families with children added to the melee. I leaned on my cane and tried to keep upright as I was jostled here and there. Even when school is not in session it is definitely a city for young people. I finally approached the beautiful chapel.

Living in England all these years I have visited many cathedrals, but this was a unique experience. Built in the fifteenth century, originally planned by King Henry VI, its medieval stained-glass windows and Ruben's Adoration of the Magi behind the altar are breathtaking. The eighty-foot-high ceiling features the world's largest fan vault, an inspiring sight.

One marvels at such extraordinary beauty created during such a dark and deadly period of British history. The Reformation spreading from Europe to Britain seemed to cause ever more suspicion, intolerance, persecution, and ultimately tens of thousands of executions "in the name of Christ." The light lit by Martin Luther and a few others appeared to produce more hatred and evil than that which came from the regime they were seeking to expose. Sectarian hostility led to betrayals between friends and within families, and tortures and executions became commonplace.

Men of God such as Sir Thomas More, Archbishop Cranmer, Ridley, and Latimer were cruelly tortured and executed for defying the monarch of the moment. More was killed at the behest of a Protestant—Henry VIII; the Oxford Martyrs were killed few decades later by a Catholic—Queen Mary. Many walked to their death because they were on the wrong side of the debate about whether Christ's "real presence" was in the Eucharist. Men waged wars concerning biblical texts, yet none considered the words of Jesus to "love your enemies" as well as your brothers.

But in the midst of hatred, suspicion, and executions, the second most beautiful book in the world appeared: Cranmer's *Book of Common Prayer.* How could that God-breathed jewel of a book come into being surrounded by such corruption? Even Cranmer himself conspired against other clergymen that he felt deserved death. And yet he proclaimed God "the author of peace and lover of concord"!

I sat there, wondering at the terrible period in which that beautiful church was erected, and recalled Pastor Latimer's words as he was being consumed by flames: "We shall this day, by God's grace, light up such a candle in England as, I trust, will never be put out."

That light of Christ's gospel may have flickered during the worst of times, but even in this secular twenty-first century the light of Christ burns powerfully in the hearts of many of His followers. We may feel overwhelmed with godlessness all around us, but He has promised never to leave us! As I left the chapel and rejoined the throng of laughing and shouting tourists and locals, I knew that He was even that day reviving hearts to know Him.

But my old legs were giving out, and I had to sit down. There was a patch of space on the wall in front of the chapel, and I gratefully sank down on it. A middle-aged woman was sitting to my right, and she smiled and greeted me. It didn't take a minute before we were engaged in conversation. Anne was a new widow, revisiting the city her late husband loved. It was a poignant time for her, less comforting than she had hoped it would be.

I was able to commiserate, recalling Tony's love for Oxford. It was as natural as breathing to tell her of my love for Jesus Christ—my Redeemer, my Deliverer, my everything. She responded that she had not been a churchgoer in recent years, but had attended as a child. She freely admitted that she badly needed direction at this time of her life. I encouraged her to simply ask God to show her His way for her. Before we parted, I asked if I might pray with her, and she readily agreed. Sitting on the wall in front of King's Chapel, I asked the Lord to shine His light into her life and bring her His peace. We hugged and kissed each other and I left.

I walked a few more blocks in the direction of Silver Street and my bus stop. I noted an open door at a small church named St. Bodolph's, and I eagerly entered. They were serving coffee and displaying books and other items. I looked over at the pew filled with paperback books and to my joy found one I had lost decades earlier and had never replaced. Roy Hession's *Calvary Road*, the book that had meant so much to me in the 1960s when we lived in the New York area. I had loaned it to a friend, and that was the last time I saw it. Now here it was in a church bookstall, priced at fifty pence. A bargain! It would be wonderful to read it again.

That evening back in our hotel room I once more responded to Roy Hession's challenging appeal. I thought how our own lives are not unlike the history of a nation. We go through dark and sinful times in desperate need of revival, but the light of Christ still glows in the darkest of places, and His mercy and grace are ever available when we seek Him.

On Sunday Sue and I boarded a double-decker touring bus, getting a bird's-eye view of that ancient city. Finally we climbed off at Fitzwilliam Museum to explore the paintings, books, and artifacts in that vast place. Dear Sue insisted on grabbing a wheelchair and placing my weary bones in it. I appreciated the masterpieces so much more from that vantage point.

Sitting across from her at lunch, I once again felt the thrill of our discovery of each other all those years ago. Despite the intervening years, that blessing was still as fresh and new as it was that day in July 1984, when that Scripture in Isaiah 54 touched my heart and gave me a gentle warning that something was about to happen. Now as I looked at my daughter who was no longer young, still to me she appeared to be the twenty-nine-year-old girl of our first meeting.

We were talking about Tommy Zeigler. Some weeks earlier I had felt directed to write a letter about him to Pope Francis, who has proven to be a real champion of people in difficulties. Tommy was raised as a Southern Baptist, but while in prison he met a Catholic chaplain who took such an interest in him that Tommy began to inquire about the Catholic faith. He converted some years before I became acquainted with him, and he is now a devout Catholic Christian. I could not imagine any other appeal more worthy of Pope Francis's intervention than Tommy's. When I approached the twenty members of Tommy's international supporters committee, they encouraged me to write and ask for his help.

Sue and a number of other supporters wrote their own letters to Pope Francis, and we hoped we would receive a reply. We knew he must receive many thousands of letters asking for his help and blessing, but I was stubborn enough to believe that Tommy's case was so tragic that he could not overlook it.

Tommy's latest letter had appeared in my mailbox the morning we left for Cambridge, and in it he mentioned his prayers for my visit to the surgeon and for our trip to Cambridge that weekend. Tommy carries on lively correspondence with dozens of friends and appears to live his life through their activities and associations.

Tommy ended his letter with these words:

> Take care, dear friend, and please keep me in your thoughts and prayers, and know you and yours are in mine. My best to the family. God bless and keep you and yours in His loving care.
>
> Sincerely, Tommy

From Cambridge we drove back north avoiding motorways and passing through villages and beautiful countryside, finally arriving in Stratford-upon-Avon for the night. We stayed, of course, at the ancient half-timbered Shakespeare Hotel, a short walk away from Shakespeare's birthplace. I had done the tourist bit many times over the years, so I was happy to rest my feet the following day and let Sue take in all the town's most famous landmarks. We arrived back in Cheshire that evening.

Although I was happy to drive Sue thither and yon during the two weeks of her visit, I also had a lengthy list of computer problems I was hoping she could solve! I could not imagine being without my computer, my laptop, or my most recent acquisition, an iPad; so when something went wrong, I was devastated. My computer expertise ends with my ability to type on the keyboard. But there were a half-dozen problems needing more expert experience, including an unpredictable Wi-Fi, and a gremlin in my iPad that seemed to delight in rejecting my passwords. I was thrilled that she so easily and expertly dealt with my many complaints. She was a marvel.

The morning after our return to Cheshire, Sue and I went

around the corner to the home of my friends Mike and Kath Blears. I had told them so much about my daughter, and I often described to Sue the wonderful progress being made at the school they founded in Kenya. Kath showed us the latest pictures of the new classrooms recently erected, the new teacher added to expand the student body, and the beautiful smiling faces of the eighty boys and girls who loved their school and adored Papa Mike and Momma Kath.

Among the many friends waiting to see Sue was my dear sister Philomena, who was now semiretired at the convent in Wales in which she had ministered as Mother Superior for many years. Although in her mideighties and with some painful health problems, she continued to serve the sisters there in a variety of ways.

When Sue first came into my life back in the 1980s, Philo was Mother Superior to the Altrincham Loreto Convent, just across the street from our home, Copperfield. Philo was one of my first friends to meet Sue when she arrived in England to meet the family. Philo had also met up with Sue in California when she flew out there to visit her brother and family who also lived in the Los Angeles area. So Philo was an old friend to us both.

We drove the seventy miles from my home to Llandudno, North Wales, and joined the sisters for Mass after which we had lunch together in the dining room. I almost feel an "honorary Catholic" when I visit and greet these dear sisters, all of whom have given their lives in service to the Lord Jesus Christ and His Church. Now, in their eighties and nineties, they are themselves being served by loving hands of other, younger women.

After lunch Philo, Sue, and I traveled along the Dee Estuary past the exquisite Bodnant Gardens and into the tiny village of

Llanrwst. Cars must traverse a very narrow humpback bridge, single file, to get to the other side of the river to enjoy a beautiful Welsh tea at a fifteenth-century tearoom. This charming cottage is completely covered with bright red Virginia Creeper in the autumn season, and as we approached, it was ablaze with fall colors. Indoors is a heavily beamed tearoom with oak tables and chairs and a large fireplace that fills one wall. Blue and white plates decorate the walls, and brass jugs and tankards that hang from the beams. Waitresses serve hot scones with clotted cream and jam and of course tea in teapots (never tea bags) making a memorable afternoon.

I feel it is a particular pleasure, each time I visit Sister Philo, to pray with and for her, as she prays with and for me. We have come a long way together, and for almost forty years we have learned to understand each other and the different backgrounds from which we have come. But the more we learn about each other, the closer we become. As I read about the terrible history of Catholic-Protestant conflict in Britain and Ireland, I feel so sad that while both traditions claimed to own and read the Word of God, they failed to read the instruction—"He who does not love does not know God" (1 John 4:8). And still today many "Christians" fail to heed this!

Our last dinner guests before Sue's visit came to a close were my friends Owen and Jayne Lowery. I had met forty-six-year-old Owen when he was just eighteen, the same year his neck was broken in that judo accident. In recent years one of his caretakers, a pretty nurse named Jayne, was especially attentive to him, and we were all surprised and delighted when they announced they were to marry. Last year, in an open-air ceremony in the

Lake District, in a bird sanctuary, they said their vows.

We all knew that Jayne was taking on incredible responsibilities. Often in past years, when Owen visited me for lunch, there were two or three caretakers to look after him, drive the van, help him in and out of his seat, and tend to his many needs. These days Jayne alone, hardly more than five feet tall, adeptly straps him into his chair, wheels him to the van, calls down the lift, pushes him onto it and raises it, then hooks and straps his chair securely into place. Then she swings around to the front and leaps up into the driver's seat and takes off. On her own. What a woman! We are all very happy that they have found their soul mates at this time of their lives.

Owen has recently begun traveling to major cities to give poetry readings from his latest published book. He will be awarded his doctor's degree next year. One of his daily pleasures is to write a poem on a general subject and also to write a poem to Jayne each day. After his last visit to me here at Beech Lawn, he surprised me by emailing me a beautiful poem describing God's artistic gift to me that day on a Yorkshire hillside:

A Gift From God

> The colour of His touch bursts
> a moment with a field of clusters,
> each of which deserves
> as much of the praise
> you've been saving, becoming a first
> time, an amazement
>
> born of nothing or something
> more than itself, a coming
> to terms with whatever summons

the delicate mechanics
into art, gets you humming
to that note the making

rings inside, echoing
when you respond from the next
gift of breath, selecting
Artist from the names
you could have chosen for perfection
found like a flame,

burning still when your fingers
work a page to the single
image left tingling
in the field behind you,
channeling the spark, the sting
you'll keep as a reminder.

Owen, 27 August, 2014

After our busy days visiting with friends and seeing sights around Cheshire, it was good for Sue and me to sit down together quietly and reminisce about all that had happened to us in the years apart—as well as the years we have spent together.

I was telling her about the time a mother came to me to ask for help and advice for her daughter who was pregnant and wanted to get an abortion. What should she do, she asked me. From my own experience, I said, I would advise her to have the child and give it to a childless couple who were longing to have one of their own. At the same time, I said, that waiting period could be valuable for her to consider the choices she had made, to pray that God would in the future direct her to His choices, and to learn to surrender to Him. If she took the easy way out, I thought, she might not give herself the opportunity to consider His will.

As it turned out, the mother agreed with me, but the daughter did not. She had an abortion and I did not hear that she had subsequently sought God's way in her life.

I had not, at that time, known that God was going to put my daughter back into my life just a short time afterward!

I asked Sue, "Have you ever felt resentful that I deserted you, and gave you up to another family?"

"No, no . . . I never felt that. I believed that God placed me in the family that needed me. Abe and Betty often quarreled, and even when I was young, I thought that I was keeping them together. Even though they eventually divorced, I believe that they stayed together all those years because of their love for me. I knew I was an important, even central, point in their lives. They would have been very lonely without me!"

Both Sue and I believe the old adage "everything happens for a purpose." But I do not accept this in a fatalistic way. I believe this is true only under one condition—"to those who love God, to those who are the called according to His purpose" (Rom. 8:28).

I told her about how my brother-in-law, Don, chided me many years earlier when I was learning to "praise God in *all* circumstances." I had been telling him that having Sue was the best thing that could have happened to me, as it brought me to Christ. He argued that I should not rejoice in *sin*, as God could have just as easily brought me back in another way. I believed then—and now—that He was willing to take that act and turn it into the means of me surrendering to Him.

I remembered a Bible study on Psalm 139 I had given to a women's group not long after Sue and I had been reunited. I took with me a needlepoint canvas I had been working on that month. It was almost finished, and it was going to be an exquisite display of flowers and colors. As I held it up to show the group, there were oohs and aahs in admiration. Then I turned the frame over, to show a confusing jumble of wools in clashing colors and no design whatsoever. I said, "That is often the picture of incomprehensible events in our lives, things that make no sense at the time, and we wonder where God is in it all!"

In Isaiah 54, that prophecy that God used so powerfully with me in July 1984, the verse that touched me then and forever after is this: "For a small moment have I forsaken thee; but with great mercies will I gather thee. In a little wrath I hid my face from thee for a moment; but with everlasting kindness will I have mercy on thee" (vv. 7–8 KJV).

At times when nothing makes sense, don't we feel that God is hiding His face from us? But even then, He is working out His purposes.

That night Sue and I held each other and tears flowed, but not from sorrow of lost years. They were tears of understanding, of our learning to grasp something of God's wonderful, merciful, loving, amazing grace!

The final Sunday of Sue's visit I was happy to take her to my dear church home—St. Mary's parish church in Bowdon. It is much more than a beautiful building, although it is certainly that. It is first of all God's house, and the ministry team are devoted servants of the Lord. It is, as is sometimes said about a special person, "beautiful inside as well as outside."

From the first note played by the organ, I felt the blessing of God upon us. That wonderful choir proceeded down the center aisle: children, young people, and adults robed in purple and white following the cross and bearer. We all sang "Let all the world in ev'ry corner sing, My God and King" from a that inspiring sixteenth-century poet George Herbert. What a powerful beginning to our worship!

In typical Anglican tradition, Scripture readings were given—Epistles first, then the Gospels—before which the people rose to the command: "The Word of the Lord!" This signifies quite rightly the pre-eminence of the words of Jesus our Savior and Lord Who was and is and always will be the Word of God.

The Epistle reading was from the beginning of Romans 12, where the apostle Paul appeals to believers to present our bodies as a living sacrifice. The Gospel portion was from the first chapter of John's gospel, where John the Baptist sees Jesus approach and exclaims: "The Lamb of God Who takes away the sins of the world!" (v.29) And when men inquire about Him, He says, "Come and see" (v.26).

The anthem "Holy, Holy, Holy" was sung by the choir with spectacular power and beauty, after which Father Gordon Herron rose to deliver the homily. He based his sermon on the theme *Pilgrim*, describing life as a pilgrimage which we all walk in one way or another. He used the text "Come and see!" to challenge his listeners to place themselves in that ancient spot before the Master who urges all in these last days to turn to Him.

Father Gordon referred to the baptism ceremony when godparents are asked (in the place of the child) "Do you turn to Christ?" He confessed that this is done according to church canon, but the clergy is often forcing the new parents and godparents to perjure themselves before God, when many make promises at these ceremonies who have no faith. The clergy asks, "Do you turn to Christ? Do you resist the Devil?" and many, thinking of the ceremony as a pleasant social gathering instead in important spiritual one, agree without thinking about it.

Father Gordon pleaded with his listeners: "Turn away, right around, to face Christ—if you dare!" He said, "We strive for reconciliation, but we cannot have this until we face the need of repentance."

He continued: "Yes, there's the creed, the theology, the doctrine, and the prayers of the Church of England but the absolute essential is this: Do we have a personal relationship with Jesus Christ?"

As we were about to take Holy Communion, we all prayed that wonderful expression of humble access:

> We do not presume to come to this Thy table,
>   merciful Lord,
> trusting in our own righteousness, but in Thy manifold
>   and great mercies.

And once again I thought of the last time Tony and I were given Communion, the weekend before he died. But it was not a sad thought; it was one of remembering our great blessings.

After Communion we sang that beautiful declaration of faith:

> Lord Jesus Christ, I would come to You,
> Live my life for You, Son of God!
> All Your commands I know are true;
> Your many gifts will make me new
> Into my life Your power breaks through,
>   Living Lord!

As the choir left the stalls and recessed back up the aisle, we sang a hymn from the seventeenth-century poet Richard Baxter, whose final verse was particularly appropriate for me as I face an uncertain future:

Let all thy days
Till life shall end
Whate'er He send
Be filled with praise!

But however uncertain, it is a wonderful future! "Whether we live or die, we are the Lord's" (Rom. 14:8).

Many years ago, at a party, we were all asked the question: "Who are you? Give me three answers." I think at the time, foolish girl that I was, I said something like this: "My name is Vicki, I am a singer, and I want to be a fashion designer."

Years later I reviewed that question and had three very different answers. "I am a new creature in Christ, and I am a wife and a mother."

Now at this time in my life, I might alter those answers once more. "I love my God and Savior with all my heart, soul, and mind. I am a mother, grandmother, and great-grandmother. And my name is Vera Ruth Weiss Holland."

Some of us go through life proud of the names we inherited from our families and even proud of the name chosen for us at birth. Such people often work diligently to make their families proud and continue the traditions that have been carried down through the generations. Some others can't wait to cast off the names that limit them in various ways—they are eager to reinvent themselves. Certainly I was guilty of that during my teen years.

But over the past six decades I have been looking at life through different eyes. I study the Scriptures and am learning an overwhelming fact: God loved me so much He even had His eye on me before I was born! "Fear not, . . . I have called you by your name; you are Mine" (Isa. 43:1). And now I wonder, when He put my name in His Book of Life, what name did He write? I begin to think that perhaps He meant me to have the name Vera after all.

When my sister and I were young, we enjoyed reading a booklet of boys' and girls' names and deciding which names we would want to name our children. But during one of many squabbles, I sought out the name *Irene* in the booklet and crossed out the meaning, *one who brings peace,* and wrote instead *one who is always fighting.* The next time I picked up the booklet, I happened to note beside my name, *Vera,* that the meaning, *one who is truthful,* had been crossed out, and in its place was scribbled, *one who is always lying.* Oh dear!

But the name Vera does mean veritas or truth, and as I have lived in God's truth all these sixty years, in the blessed wonder of Jesus, the way, the truth, and the life, I begin to cherish that old-fashioned name that I discarded so long ago. Recently a friend who did not know my official name was surprised when I confessed it to her. "Why, it's a beautiful name!" she said, and from that moment I began to believe it.

Even my middle name, *Ruth,* has become more precious to me over the years. It was the name of a godly woman, who left her own country to remain with her widowed mother-in-law and who became an ancestor of our Lord Jesus. Her book and story is a beloved portion of the Bible. In fact, for our wedding ceremony in 1958, I asked the pastor to include the passage from Ruth 1:16: "Entreat me not to leave you, or to turn back from following after you, for wherever you go, I will go; and wherever you lodge, I will lodge; Your people shall be my people, and your God, my God." And it was my privilege and joy to return with Tony to the land of his birth nine years later, which became my cherished home as well.

Ruth also was the name of my dear mentor, Ruth Schwenk, whose godly life and counsel meant the world to me over the years.

So perhaps my father was not just obliging a stranger in giving me the name that God had already written in His Book of Life! And if so, who am I to change it?

BIBLIOGRAPHY

Augustine of Hippo, *Confessions*. Harmondsworth, Middlesex: Penguin Books Ltd., 1961.

Carre, E. G. (ed), *Praying Hyde,* Gainesville, Florida: Bridge-Logos, 1982.

Dirks, Walter, *Salt of the Earth.* Trowbridge, Wiltshire: Eagle Publishing, 2002.

Dostoyevsky, Fyodor, *The Brothers Karamazov.* Harmondsworth, Middlesex: Penguin Books Ltd., 1958.

Edersheim, Alfred, *Jesus the Messiah.* Peabody, Mass.: Hendrickson Publishers Inc., 1993.

Edman, V. Raymond, *They Found the Secret.* Grand Rapids, Mich.: Zondervan, 1960.

Guyon, Madame, *The Autobiography of Madame Guyon.* Chicago: Moody Press, 1955.

Hession, Roy, *The Calvary Road.* Alresford, Hampshire: Christian Literature Crusade, 1950.

Kazantzakis, Nikos, *Christ Recrucified,* London: Faber & Faber, 1962.

Kempis, Thomas à, *Imitation of Christ.* New York: Grosset and Dunlap, 1976.

Lawson, James Gilchrist, *Deeper Experiences of Famous Christians.* Anderson, Ind.: Gospel Trumpet Company, 1911.

Lewis, C. S., *Mere Christianity.* Hammersmith, London: Harper Collins, 1950.

MacCullock, Diarmaid, *Thomas Cranmer*. New Haven, Conn.: Yale University Press, 1996.

MacDonald, George, *The Wind from the Stars*. London: Harper Collins, 1992.

Merton, Thomas, *The Seven Storey Mountain*. London: SPCK, 2009.

Metaxas, Eric, *Bonhoeffer: Pastor, Martyr, Prophet, Spy*. Nashville, Tenn.: Thomas Nelson, 2010.

Miura, Ayako, *Shiokari Pass*. Sevenoaks, Kent: Overseas Missionary Fellowship, 1974.

Nee, Watchman, *The Normal Christian Life*. Eastbourne: Kingsway, 2005.

Pierson, Arthur T. *George Muller of Bristol*. Peabody, Mass.: Hendrickson Publishers, 2008.

Schlink, Basilia, *Behold His Love*. Basingstoke, Hampshire: Lakeland, 1973.

Spurgeon, C. H., *Spurgeon's Sermons (Vol.1-10)*, New York: Robert Carter & Brothers, 1883.

Tada, Joni Eareckson, *Pearls of Great Price*, Grand Rapids, Mich.: Zondervan, 2006.

Thiessen, John Caldwell, *A Survey of World Missions*. Chicago: Intervarsity Press, 1955.

Wati, I. Ben, *My Early Years: Nagaland 1920–35*. Guwahati, India: Council of Baptist Churches, 2008.

Wenger, J. C., ed., *The Complete Writings of Menno Simon*. Scottsdale, Penn.: Herald Press, 1956.

Wesley, John, *The Journals*. London: C. H. Kelly, 1891.

Wurmbrand, Richard, *In God's Underground*. London: Hodder and Stoughton, 1966.

Yan, Brother, *The Heavenly Man*. Mill Hill, London: Monarch Books, 2002.

AFTERWORD

That moment on a Yorkshire hillside many years ago (page 95) when I praised the Lord for being such an awesome artist, a chain of events began that still amazes me. A day or two later, almost without thinking, I bought an art pad and pencils and sat down in the middle of the village to sketch the scene before me.

Within a few months I found myself doing house portraits, first for friends and eventually accepting commissions for other homeowners, and eventually doing sketches for hotels and public buildings.

I wasn't sure where this was going until an elderly friend, Hyldia Shepherd, asked me to write and design some tracts for her. Even though she was unable to get around easily, she used every opportunity to share the gospel with other residents in her nursing home, or even to strangers when she was taken shopping.

She complained to me that the tracts she had seemed too old-fashioned. We both felt that our first tract or pamphlet was a gift from the Lord, the greatest Artist of all!

Something Beautiful . . .

As an artist, I find great
beauty in the homes of
England. I love to do
house portraits of houses
and buildings of every description: thatched-roof
cottages . . . half-timbered
inns . . . rambling Victorian houses . . . homes great or small.

But there is something far more beautiful and important
in my life than that. It is being surrounded by the work of the
greatest Artist of all time . . .

Rembrandt? Michelangelo? No; the greatest Artist is the
One Who gave them that extraordinary talent: God Himself.
He is the One Who formed this fabulous limitless universe and
the resources to sustain our lives . . .

*When I consider thy heav-
ens, the work of thy fingers,
the moon and the stars which
thou hast ordained, what is
man, that thou art mindful
of him* (Psalm 8:3–4)

The greatest Artist is the One Who fashioned man with billions
of atoms . . . Who created in each a magnificent cell structure,
nervous system and blood supply . . . yet every human being is
so utterly unique that no two have identical fingerprints . . .

*I will praise thee, for I am fearfully and wonderfully made:
marvelous are thy works, and that my soul knoweth right well.*
(Psalm 139:14)

He is the One who puts precious patterns in every snowflake and each field flower. Not a blade of grass escapes His beautiful touch . . .

Consider the lilies of the field, how they grow. They toil not, neither do they spin. And yet I say unto you that even Solomon in all his glory was not arrayed like one of these. **(Matthew 6:28–29)**

The greatest Artist is the One who can take a life of mistakes and misery, sin and sorrow, and transform it into a new creature in Christ! I know; it happened to me!

I will put my law in their inward parts, and write it in their hearts, and will be their God, and they shall be my people . . . for I will forgive their iniquity, and I will remember their sin no more. **(Jeremiah 31:33–34)**

I didn't always know God as I do now. I knew He was there, but I wanted to live my own life. Like many people today, I was a created being who refused to follow the 'manufacturer's instructions' and, not surprisingly, broke down . . .

The greatest Artist is the One Who let His Son be mocked, betrayed, beaten, and executed—and made something beautiful of that!

He that spared not his own son, but delivered him up for us all, how shall He not with Him also freely give us all things? **(Romans 8:32)**

If you cannot say that God has done something beautiful in your life, won't you give yourself to Him now? What could be better than surrendering your life and future to the Lord Who loves you so much?

Vicki Holland
COPPERFIELD PRINTS

ACKNOWLEDGMENTS

I want to express my deep gratitude to an old friend, Bob Brinkerhoff, who worked with my late husband all those years ago on the Dove project at Lever Brothers. We rejoiced when Bob came to faith in Christ and joined us in worshiping at Grace Chapel in New Jersey.

I could not have imagined then that decades later his son Paul would become a dear friend and brother in Christ through our email correspondence. Paul, who was himself in Christian publishing ministry, later introduced me to his friend and mentor, Tim Beals, of Credo House Publishers. I am so very much indebted to these three Christian men for their support and encouragement as I told my story.

I also want to thank my cousin Kate Brown Treick for her editing and proofing in the early stages of this project, and to thank my favorite journalist Gail Hollenbeck for her wise counsel at the later stages. And special thanks and love to my daughter Susan Joseph Kientz for her help with a multitude of computer problems and issues with photos and illustrations. I couldn't have done this without you, Sue!

But of course, all of these dear people, and others, are just God's instruments. As am I.